I Am Her

◇◇◇◇◇◇◇◇◇◇◇◇◇◇◇◇◇◇◇◇◇◇◇◇◇◇◇◇◇◇◇◇◇◇◇◇◇◇

MESSY, FLAWED, AND LOVED BY GOD

GABRIELLE ELISCO

ISBN 978-1-0980-5698-8 (paperback)
ISBN 978-1-0980-5997-2 (hardcover)
ISBN 978-1-0980-5699-5 (digital)

Christian Faith Publishing, Inc.
832 Park Avenue
Meadville, PA 16335
www.christianfaithpublishing.com

Printed in the United States of America

To Jesus Christ,
the Lover of my soul.
May all I do honor and glorify You.

CONTENTS

INTRODUCTION

Hey there, pretty girl!

So you've just opened the page of a brand-new book, and you've probably wondered a few things before doing so. First, "Who is *her?*" Second, "What am I going to gain out of reading this book?" Well, I'm glad you've asked.

Let me begin by introducing myself. I am *you.* Did I just confuse you? I apologize. Allow me to elaborate. You see, we gals have got much more in common, perhaps even more than we've previously realized. Let's set aside the constant race of comparison and keeping up with the Kardashians and all of their look-alikes, and we've got ourselves some familiar ground here. I, you, and all of the other women around us are an unfinished work. We've got our strengths and our awesomeness, and then we have our flaws and kind of messiness. But there's been a trend during these past few decades, and emerged the plight of striving for perfectionism to appear to the masses. I'll bet an entire meteor shower heading toward planet Earth at this very moment that you've suffered from this phenomenon too. Please don't peek out of your window for the sky to fall. I can be a bit dramatic at times.

Anyway, we live in a society where either you must have the coveted social media page or you've mastered a start-up business from your garage that brings in more revenue than your college degree ever could. Polaroid pictures are now outdated by Photoshop presets, and you're below basic if you have less than three thousand followers on the gram (will the real millennials please stand up?). Women throughout the country, throughout the world, are increasingly obsessed with displaying their staged lives, with their perfect house, perfect body, perfect man, and perfect talent, that we've actually adapted the mind-set that everyone around us is without flaw. That excludes ourselves of course. I bought into that ideology entirely. I too coveted the "plastics" wondering how they obtained that lifestyle and what on earth was I doing so wrong that I wasn't a part of that desired population too? But then I grew suspicious, and I got tired of it all. I became repulsed and rather exhausted with having to show the world that I have a doting fiancé who sends me flowers for no reason at all or that I can hand paint a wooden sign and sell it on Etsy. I grew utterly annoyed with the fact that I now needed a specific filter to keep my Instagram pictures in perfect synchronicity. That's. Not. Real. Life. But here's what is.

I'm a mess—and not in a negative, self-demeaning way. In fact, I love who I am, because I fought incredibly hard to become her. But I'm not perfect, and I am millions of lightyears away from it. I am a recovered obsessive planner and constant comparer who got divorced at twenty-seven years old. I've had a temper since I was a toddler and have a wick of patience so minuscule that it need be examined only via microscope. So having said that, what makes me so special or qualified enough to educate you on discovering your true potential? Why me? I'm not a life coach, nor do I have a prerequisite for counseling or a PhD in theology. I don't have a twelve-step program to boost you along your way, nor did I innovate something as iconic as the five love languages (shout-out to you, Gary Chapman). Here's what I am, though.

I am a woman who has wasted years of my life hating myself. I wasted day after day, night after night, striving to be someone I am not so that people would approve that falsified version of who I am. And with a heavy heart, I'm willing to bet you've been there too. So I decided that I would be transparent with the world, or with whomever was gracious enough to purchase a copy of this book, and tell you a bit about me—the real me and not just that I love tacos and puppies or that I have hyperextended thumbs. I want to talk about the messy, annoying, unattractive parts of myself, ones that we may have in common so we can relate with one another. I want to help you go from loathing the pieces that compose you and how they've hindered you to discovering a love and acceptance for yourself you've never before known. And while doing so, I'm probably going to tell you some sad, embarrassing, and often funny stories about myself that I'll be sharing for the first time. I know you and I have a totally different story, but I'm gutsy enough to bet that some of our chapters look a bit familiar. I'll also dare to believe that like me, you've spent a bit too much time concealing your undesirable parts rather than accentuating your awesome ones. That's where that nasty devil likes to torment ya. He encourages you to focus on the failures in efforts to snuff out the talents and gifts God has given you, because if he can wear you down and knock you out, you become ineffective in the kingdom of God. But, sis, that's up to you and only you. I can encourage until I have nothing left to pour into you, and I can walk alongside holding your hand in baby steps, but only you can take off running. And like anything else in this life, it's a marathon, not a sprint. I do not anticipate after you close the back cover of this book that you'll have it all figured out. I wrote it, and guess what? I'm not even close to having life "figured out." None of us are. But it's a journey we take together, step by step, and the best part of it is that we aren't doing it alone.

I want to touch hearts with you, imperfect sister, who braves to show the world the lowlights just as much as the highlights. What if instead of racing with the world around us, we dared to be proud enough of ourselves to not care if it sees the real us? I'm not just talking about some cliché version of telling you to be yourself or take a makeup wipe to your face and post a selfie without your bronzer. I want to resonate with the anxious heart, the meek, the hurt, the shamed, and the work in progress and encourage you to love and find value in every ounce of your being. To the girl who feels less than, the girl who feels uncool, unaccepted, and flawed from the inside out, I'm speaking to you who feel like you have absolutely nothing to bring to the table and can't stand in the heels of Miss Suzy Homemaker. To the girl who was told she meant nothing and the world would be just fine without her, I am here to tell you that's a boldface lie from the pit of hell. You matter. You are more than what they've told you and much more than what you've convinced yourself to believe too. It doesn't matter how many times you've made a mess of things in the past; it means nothing regarding your background or where you've come from or what you can and cannot do. God put you on this planet for a reason. And when He breathed life into your lungs, He reigned purpose over your existence. He set into motion a destiny specifically tailored for you in this great big world. He gave you feet to move and hands to reach. You have a voice for hurting ears and a heart with a custom passion that only you can offer to others the way He intended. You've been given everything you need to succeed in this life. He's just waiting for you to believe it. And so am I.

Now let's begin together, sis, and discover who we are and what we have to give back to this great, big, beautiful life. In each chapter, we are going to take a walk through some of the parts of myself that I've struggled with most. Some things we will go over a dozen times to ensure that they've saturated your mind. At the conclusion of each chapter, you'll find some crucial points to take away with you and my challenge for you to come up with your very own "I Am Her" statement. Watch out, world. Here we come.

Oh and by the way, now that we're friends, you can call me Gabby.

In His love always,
xoxo

CHAPTER 1
The Self-Hater

I praise you because I am fearfully and wonderfully
made; your works are wonderful,
I know that full well.
—Psalm 139:14 (NIV)

There will always be someone who can't see
your worth. Don't let it be you.
—Mel Robbins

My expertise on eyebrows is equivalent to a toddler mastering trigonometry. Seriously.

I do not understand how to shape them and fill them. Like, what does all of that even mean? I truthfully cannot even grasp the phenomenon overtaking the eyebrow world by storm. Quite frankly, I'm not even sure what my eyebrows are supposed to look like or if they are even acceptable the way they are. I would more likely find proper usage out of using an eyebrow pencil as a writing utensil than something to darken the little hairs above my eyes with. Do you want to know what my maintenance concerning my eyebrow area is? I get a razor, line it directly between my two eyebrows, press to skin, and slide on down. In shorter terms, I don't pluck; I shave. And I won't lie. This chick is susceptible to a unibrow. As far as the other little stragglers under my brows, they either get left there, or I would have an occasional twice-a-year pluck if I'm feeling fresh. You eyebrow connoisseurs just quivered a little, didn't you? Let me be more honest with you. There are evenings I fall asleep without washing the three layers of attempted contouring off of my face or a day I skip shaving my legs and still rock some shorts, and more than often do I go to work without a stitch of makeup on. Be easy now. I'm not a disgusting excuse for a woman, I promise. The truth is, though, I'm not always put together, I'm not always dressed to impress, and I'm not on a Pinterest fashion inspirational board. I'm just real. Some days I could not possibly care less about the way that I look, and other days I feel inspired enough to paint my lips red and foolishly attempt false eyelashes. This is me. And I am confident with her. Oh and by the way, that last sentence you just read there, well, it took about twenty-some years to muster up.

I have never, let me repeat never (one last time, never), been confident with my appearance. Never. Did you get that? Just making sure. I have been insecure about my nose, the scar on my right cheek, my smile, the mole on my back, and the scars from acne remaining on my shoulders—and that's just a few to say the least. I did not like—rather, I despised—those parts of my physical being. They are gross, unattractive, and rather disgusting in my opinion. But we are more than just our outward appearances, right? I mean that's what has been beaten into our heads since junior high school. You know, that inner beauty we all rave about, because that's what we've been conditioned to say is what really matters. Well, that part was even uglier to me. I hated how I was constantly nervous, panicked, short-tempered, compulsive, and obsessive. The way I was wired and composed to be put together just did not make sense to me at all. I did not understand me. How I just wished I could change or even trade these ugly parts with someone else for their more desirable ones. I spent my entire life disliking those facets of myself so incredibly much that I went out of my way to conceal them. I'd wear glasses more than often to make my nose appear smaller or to disguise the bump on the right side of it. I would sit in the classroom at school from elementary spelling to college gerontology class with my right hand pressed against my right cheek to cover the scar on my face. My educators must have presumed I was rather bored by their teachings. I put on the fake smile and appeared to be "okay" with friends and co-workers and in romantic relationships because if anyone knew how much work I really was, would they even love me? Would they truly believe I was worthy of their time? I was constantly aware of being sure that I was tending to mask the parts of myself that I so strongly disliked that I forgot to cater to the parts that I actually wasn't too repulsed by. I fed the insecurities and starved the gifts.

Do we have anything in common, yet? If you are a self-confident rock star and you live life actually recognizing yourself for how awesome you really are, hats off to you, my sister. I offer you my round of applause. But chances are, if we're being honest with ourselves, you too could find some scratch paper and a pen, or eyebrow pencil if you are like me, and compose a list of the things you'd like to alter on your body. We're women, and sadly, that's what we do.

Living in a world today that has so many demands that are barricading us with expectations for perfectionism is incomprehensibly difficult. We are shown from a young age what the definition of beauty should resemble, and quite honestly, it could not be more far off. How do we tame the definition of beautiful when there are so many different eyes that behold it? How do we conceptualize something that's truly unmeasurable? It's a universal entity, and we all have various perceptions of what we depict to be attractive. Jan may covet your long legs, but Jodi is into the more petite, short look. Sally wishes so badly she had your compact curls, but Susan longs for straight hair that doesn't require ten ounces of serum each morning to contain the frizziness. There is a dangerous rage of self-disapproval in our world today because we are all entertaining this draining act of comparison and seeking validation among others. We are horrible critics to our own minds. As a society, we have become so lost, so twisted in false constructs of acceptance that we truly have no idea what direction we are heading in. The fads that are manifesting throughout the television, internet, and social media are surfacing at a faster rate than we can manage. By the end of each day, you have more than likely been convinced that you need antiaging serum that derived from the root of a beet, eyelashes so full you could dust your countertop with, or this insane device that you place around your waist that ultimately reconstructs your rib cage for a smaller circumference. Girls, we must get this under control. It is vital to our well-being. But it begins with our own selves.

Our standards and definitions of what it means to be beautiful are a dependent variable. It's ever-changing from woman to woman to woman. Yet what matters is what *you* think of beauty when you look into the mirror. *All right*, you're thinking, *here comes the cheesy pep talk about loving myself.* Well, yes and no. Let's go deeper than the second grade "be yourself" speech.

It took me nearly decades to come to the well-overdue realization to accept every ounce of being. Once I got past the stage of acceptance, I had to propel my mental state toward actually *loving* myself. (Those are two totally different concepts by the way). And do you know how I got there? It was when I was in the pit of despair, at the very base of it, when I didn't want to even live anymore. I went through a period of a dark depression when every morning that I opened my eyes, the first thought I had was that I wished I hadn't. That was a horrifying place to find myself in, but there are some lessons that you can only learn in a valley. There are some dark, devastating moments when you have to capture the only tiny beacon of light you can find and hold on to it for dear life. I do not wish that dark cove for anyone to visit, though stooping that low allowed for me to understand that I should never, ever take my heartbeat for granted, regardless of how much I loved or loathed myself. Wanting to not exist is singlehandedly one of the most terrifying notions that could fleet through the human mind; and when Jesus healed that part of me, I looked at myself, at my life, even the parts that I did not care much for, differently. In fact, the flawed parts of me were inevitably the fuel propelling my purpose. Hmm, stay with me here.

There is no other person on this earth who is going to spend as much time with you as yourself. You cannot escape you. Scary, I know, right? But it's true. By not only accepting but also by turning the tables to accentuate our defects rather than just our sparkles, perhaps we can shift this paradigm. I don't want to just encourage you to approve of yourself, but to use the very things that you disprove and turn those things into appreciation. My anxiety has been a burden to my life, yet it made me empathetic and merciful to others. My obsessive need for order has made me an extremely organized and responsible person. And the season of depression? It made me appreciate life more than I ever have before, because it's an incredibly fragile entity we take for granted every single day. As for the physical traits, check this out. I'm going to put you on the hot seat here, so hang tight.

If you are like me and don't like the way your nose is shaped, well, girl, thank God you have one. Some people through tragedy or deformity do not. Take a deep breath in, sister, because that baby is working just fine at accomplishing its intended purpose. Are you unhappy with your calves? You can walk; many can't. Don't like the extra jiggle under your arm? Yeah, I know how we gals are. I myself have some bingo wings. But you have two arms, two hands, and ten fingers that can be used for a mighty splendor in this world that only you can touch. I thank God for every part of me now because how I am is the way He intentionally and strategically designed me to be. Think of that for a moment.

Every orifice of your body was handcrafted by the same almighty God Who orchestrated this world you and I are inhabiting. That same God Who placed the stars in the sky and the lilies on the ground designed your body with every intention of how He wanted you to be. You are His grand art project. He worked hard on you. You are what He would take a picture of and hang on the refrigerator. And need we be reminded, we aren't here for ourselves; we are here for Him and for His eternal glory.

What would you do if your friend, child, or anyone dear to you made you something and took so much pride in their finished work, though when they presented it to you, you disproved it? As a social worker, I have had countless strange drawings that looked as though a crayon box threw up on a piece of crinkled white paper handed to me with so much pride from a smiling child. What if I placed that piece of heartfelt paper in my two hands as if it was contaminated and gave a stank face to that little human instead of warmly accepting their thoughtful gift? That is what we do to God. Can you imagine the offense He feels when you dissect every inch of what you hate on your body, how you wished you looked differently, or magnify all your flawed features? It troubles His heart greatly to hear His children scrutinize what He has taken great pride in.

I'll give you an example. I used to hate my smile. For real, gals, I hated it. I felt as though my entire face scrunched toward the center of the front of my head when I would as much as grin, and it disgusted me. Other people just looked so incredibly attractive when doing so. But me, I looked like the Grinch when he devised the plan to use his dog, Max, as a reindeer. Do you know what I realized, though? Most days, that's how I spread the love and warmth of my Creator. That's how I greet others, and it's the gateway to my laughter. So I am going to light it up like a sparkly sparkler on the Fourth of July.

It's hard. I won't lie to you. And I too still struggle some days not to regress back to my previous mind-set. When you've spent decades trying to morph the very things about yourself that you detest, then shifting your whole perception to love and acceptance, it's surely a challenge. And just like anything else we fall in love with, it takes time, dedication, and understanding (except puppies—that's instantaneous). Get comfortable with your imperfections. Learn how to be proud of them without anyone giving you the approval to do so. And stop. Oh, please stop this very moment, letting the World Wide Web or greater Hollywood area tell you if you've met the mark. Don't adapt to the world, girl. Let it adapt to you. Be extra, like when you ask for guacamole at Chipotle and the innocent worker fears your response explaining that the guac is an extra charge. Put a glitzy clip in your hair and rock it with your head held high. Smack on some deep purple lipstick if you feel beautiful in it and don't worry if the cashier at Walgreens thinks it looks strange. Feeling good about yourself is not about them; it's about *you*.

I wish I could be seated in front of you right now and hold your hands in mine and tell you how extremely valuable you are. That may come off rather disconnected considering I don't know you, but I know Who created you. And I also know that He makes no mistakes. I know that He sings over you with great delight. I need you to be reminded of that, to be sure of it. And that is not just something cute or sweet I conjured up to encourage you; that's the Word of God (see Zephaniah 3:17). Oftentimes, I believe we get into the habit of reading the Bible and interpreting its contents to resonate with the proverbial "you" rather than our own self. He means you, though. He is speaking of *you* when He says He will rejoice over you with singing. And He means *you* when He took up His cross and ruled that you were worth dying for.

So if I could look into your eyes today, if I could be with you and warm you in my arms with a well-needed hug, I would encourage you that it's time to look into your reflection and love the person staring back at you. You are a wonderful and mighty woman of God. Your face is detailed in the exact pattern He had in mind the moment He created you. Your smile makes Him smile. You did not just happen. You are no accident or big group of random cells and molecules compacted together. You are not here due to a simple act of nature. You were every bit thought of, deliberately planned, and modeled by the God of time and space. The only way you are going to learn to love yourself, regardless of all the reasons you'd refute not to, is to understand how God sees you and how much He loves you.

He has seen you at your absolute worst. He has seen you all dolled up, and He's seen you first thing in the morning. He watched you in the midst of your sin, in your filth, and yet He's called you His beloved. His love sought you when you hated Him. When you cursed and raised your fist at Him, He remained unmoved waiting for you to return home. When no one else thought you were worth anything, when you were considered unlovable, abandoned, and betrayed, He tenderly cared for you in the midst of your troubles—sometimes ones that you even caused on your own. His love doesn't make sense; rather, it fights every bit of logic. He loves you despite the fact that you may never love Him in return. Jesus doesn't care if He makes Himself vulnerable for you. He doesn't concern Himself with that fact that you may reject him. He doesn't anger imagining that you may deny Him, but He pursues your heart anyway. His love is not measured or defined by your actions. It's not a reciprocal kind of love. He always will extend the first hand. Every time you refused Him, every time you forgot Him, every time you removed Him to second, third, or tenth place, He remained faithful when you were faithless. He saw you, He found you then, and He finds you today, a total mess in need of a Savior. He loves you nonetheless. He looks upon you with fire in His eyes, with love in His heart, and grace on His lips. Jesus knew and *still* knows every unlovable part about you, but you never once had to go to Him and convince Him you were worth the ultimate sacrifice. He already knew you were.

So I want you to take a good, hard look in the mirror. Go find one and bring this book with you. This will be your first task on this journey with me.

I want you to look at yourself, and I want you to say this aloud. If you need to one hundred times until it sinks deep within your soul, do it. It's worth it. *You* are with it. Marinate on these words. Let them swim throughout your mind and establish refuge in your heart. Say them until you believe them:

"Wow, I am beautiful. Everything about me illuminates radiance and worth. Even the scars have composed a beautiful part of my being that I fought to heal from. I am loved, I am desired, and I am enough. What others have failed to see about me, my Savior takes great delight in. I am fearfully and wonderfully made by the Creator of true beauty in its most raw and natural form. I was told before that I was not beautiful enough, smart enough, kind enough, gentle enough, tall enough, skinny enough, or strong enough or had the right body, but what I see when I look in this mirror is a beautiful woman worth more than precious gold. I am showered in adoration and coated with an impenetrable sheath of love that was produced from a selfless sacrifice by the truest Gentleman to ever capture my heart. I am who He says I am, I will do what He says I can do, and I will love myself, not because I am perfect but because a perfect Savior loves me, more. I am His daughter, I am His treasure, and I am her."

Now breathe. Inhale, exhale. Cry joyous tears of relief if you must, and begin to believe what you are worthy of. Yes, those parts of yourself that you dislike may still be present. But we are no longer going to refer to those as flaws, rather they will hereby be considered "finishing touches." When designing a house, an office, or any room for the matter, you put together the main pieces and the functional furniture that you need, but then it's not complete. It's not unique or charming until it has those finishing touches. Like the scar on my cheek or the bump on my nose, they're just the final attributes that make me me. So the next time you take a look into the mirror, whether it be to fluff your hair or read that paragraph above again to yourself, remember that you are perfectly you, and no one in this entire world is better at it than you are.

Once you acknowledge that in your heart, when you wear the identity of Christ and His unwavering love for you, you begin to see the value He has placed upon your life. When you struggle to look into your reflection, know that He is looking back at you with admiration and acceptance, just the way you are. And if you need an extra boost, I'm willing to stand behind you with my hand on your shoulder and remind you just how beautiful you are. I just so happen to think your freckles are adorable, your red hair is super awesome, and your pear-shaped, round-shaped, or hourglass body is perfect just the way that it is. I believe that the gap between your teeth, the dimple in your chin, and whatever the shape, fill, or color of your eyebrows compliment you perfectly. You don't have to change a single thing.

Do not let anyone or anything—that includes your own self—convince you to tame your unique sparkle. It's time to stop hating everything you are not and embrace everything you are and have yet to become.

Things to remember:

- The most valuable love which is the love of God is already yours. You don't have to do a single thing to earn it.
- The best kind of respect in this world is self-respect. Focus most on gaining that right now.
- You were handmade by God with every detail fashioned in His image. Make no mistake that He makes none.
- True love of yourself begins when you see through the lens of the One Who loves you unconditionally.
- You are what God would bring to show and tell.

After reading this chapter:

Something that stuck with me is…

_____

_____

_____

_____

Something I want to challenge myself with…

_____

_____

_____

_____

This is how I am going to do it…

_____

_____

_____

_____

My I Am Her statement is…

_____

_____

_____

_____

CHAPTER 2
The Bad Christian

For all have sinned and fall short of the glory of God.
—Romans 3:23 (NIV)

There is more mercy in Christ than sin in us.
—Richard Sibbes

Ah, the day that I threw Jesus out of the window.

Alarming? It's true, though. I did in fact, quite literally, that is, throw Jesus out of the car window. I regretted it instantly. Well, almost instantly. It was a "heat-of-the-moment" response clouded by a plethora of anger and a giant dose of disgust. But shortly after I drove away leaving Jesus on the side of the road, I immediately was filled with regret at what I had symbolically just done.

The moment I saw the portrait painting "Prince of Peace" by Akiane, it captivated me immediately. If you are unfamiliar with the story *Heaven Is for Real*, I strongly advise that the film version be on your movie night lineup. Anyway, I had a small wallet-size picture of the painting that stuck with me for years. I had placed it strategically with a little help of Scotch Tape on the odometer center in my car. Various cars came and went, but Jesus was always fixated before my eyes while driving. In fact, that picture was with me in my car for so many years that the color was actually faded by the sun. Oh, and you'll like this one. One time I got pulled over by the police for an expired registration, and when the officer saw the picture of Jesus, he said, "I don't want to fight with Jesus today, so I'm going to let you off with a warning." So just so we're clear, Jesus was my forever pilot.

There were days when I cried to that picture, yelled at it, talked to it, begged for mercy, and pleaded for guidance, even days when I ripped it off and threw it in the cupholder because I felt as though He was continuously abandoning me when I didn't get what I wanted or at least what I thought I did. When that happened, though, I always found myself quickly asking the pocket-size portrait of my Savior to forgive me as I returned Him to His rightful position again. Can you imagine the poor, innocent civilians who are fortunate enough to drive beside me? Man, do they get a show. I'm a bit overemotional. Don't you think?

One morning, in the midst of one of my most difficult seasons, I found myself hysterical in my Chevrolet Trax yet again. I was crying so hard my face was raw. For the life of me, I could not understand what I was doing so wrong to be going through marital troubles so prematurely in life. I had about had it—at wits' end, exhausted, sleep deprived, fit to be tied. I needed something, or someone, to be infuriated with and take it all out on. Well, you can imagine who my fall boy was. I looked at Him with disgust knowing that He could fix my problems instantaneously, and I was filled with irrational and undirected rage. I grabbed that picture, I pressed the window button in a downward motion with all the might my left index finger held, and there He went.

As I drove off, I stared into my rearview mirror, and after the initial impulse passed, I cried even harder. Of course, I knew that I didn't legitimately "throw Jesus out"; it was just the emblematic action of letting Him depart from me that made me want to literally throw up.

Like many of my weary days or self-induced mistakes, I frantically cried to my mother about my shameful, pitiful, childish fit. She quickly calmed me by saying that we would bundle up in the morning (mind you, this was wintertime in Western Pennsylvania) and encouraged me that we would find Jesus. It's rather comical to speak of Jesus actually being in one geographical space when He is in fact omnipresent. I was convinced that due to the weather, wind, and cars traveling up and down that busy road all day and overnight, Jesus was probably in the middle of someone's yard at this point or even further. Perhaps a little birdie or squirrel was using Jesus for another intended purpose. My mind wandered wild. My mother tried to convince me that maybe that was a good thing because someone would find that pocket size of hope and learn of Jesus. She was right; maybe there was a bigger purpose. I still wanted Him back, though. And forget about ordering another copy of that portrait. No, I wanted *that* one. I wanted *my* Prince of Peace.

Sure enough the next morning, my mother asked me if I was ready to begin our scavenger hunt. I picked her up and headed toward the road where the picture would presumably lie. That particular road is a couple miles long, and I could only approximate where I was when I had done the dreaded deed. We reached a probable site and agreed we would begin there. I pulled the car over, and we crossed the busy street, and the first thing out of my negative mouth was "Mom, this is just stupid. We are never going to find it." We walked about fifteen feet, and I had a glimpse of hope. I saw a square resemblance of paper and rushed toward it saying, "Wait!" Never mind. It was the cardboard packaging for a Bic lighter. As I mustered the words to tell my mother it was a false alarm, I glanced over toward the left out of my peripheral vision where I saw a white, small, square paper with black lettering that read "Prince of Peace." My face lit up with juvenile joy, and I reached down for that blessed card stock to flip it around and see those eyes again. I exclaimed with triumph, and my mother responded with surprise. Untouched, just in the condition I had left it before it rested on the damp ground all night, He was back where He belonged again with me. The time it had taken us to park the car and locate my picture on that long road was less than two minutes. We were led exactly to where we needed to be. Success. Jesus restored and reunited to me. Case closed, happy ending, lesson learned, right? If you're getting to know me, you should know by now not exactly.

For the duration of my late teen years until, oh say, last evening, I have pegged myself to be a terrible Christian. I was double-minded and filled with doubt, had wavering faith, and was unfit to be a model of Christlike resemblance. To me, it would be nearly impossible for

God to use such a flawed, sinful woman such as myself. I would see other gals who were such wonderful role models of what a godly woman was supposed to look like, talk like, and act like; and I was the polar opposite. How He could use me, better yet, how he could *want* to use me, was beyond a mystery.

I appeared to always be throwing Jesus out of the hypothetical window. Remember I only *actually* did it once. When things didn't go my way, when I did not get what I wanted, when the time line just did not adhere to my schedule, I blamed Him to presumably be punishing me for being an unfit Christian. "I know," I would barter, "You are just making me pay because of what I did last week, huh?" I was as stable as a Styrofoam plate in a tornado. I based His blessings and mercy entirely on my performance. I assumed I must be an outstanding Christian to be in good standing with Christ. If I am anything less, I am an outsider to the kingdom, like a beggar shaking a cup pleading for droppings of charity. But aren't those the very types of people whom God has used significantly throughout history? Let's rewind time for a moment.

I believe oftentimes we regard the now ancient brethren of the Bible to be rather outdated and irrelevant because they walked this earth so many, many moons ago. For the sanctity of yours and my mind, let's examine a few of Jesus's pals. You know how you see in the movies when the superheroes come striding in and they are ever so strategically fanned out approaching toward the screen in slow motion? Picture the teen chick flicks with all the popular girls walking down the hallway in their best attire with the slow movements of their long locks bouncing off their shoulders and everyone gawking over them. You would think that's how Jesus approached the towns He entered, with His posse arranged behind Him, destiny amid their feet and ferocity in their eyes. These would have been the elite among the people of Jesus's time—the subjects of the Harvard or Columbia of Nazareth. Or so you would suspect.

When Jesus gathered His disciples, He didn't have a casting call. In Luke chapter 8 (NIV), the gospel opens with "And the twelve were with him, and also some women who had been healed of evil spirits and infirmities: Mary, called Magdalene, from whom seven demons had gone out…" Imagine this crew for a moment. Are you visualizing them entering your town? Tax collectors, a betrayer, a narc, and a woman who was previously a dwelling shelter for a legion of evil spirits. Jesus didn't recruit His team from the temple. He gathered them from the trenches. He knew their iniquities, He knew their shortcomings, and He was well aware of their flaws and wrap sheets and even the betrayal of some yet to come. They even kept screwing up long after He enlisted them. That didn't stop the ministry He prepared for them when calling them to be His selected followers. And do you know what? He has the same requirements for His expected qualifications today.

I let the enemy convince me for so many years that I was condemned, useless, and plagued by irredeemable sin. The whispers in my ear that told me I was beyond redemption kept me from seeking the calling God had on my life. Condemnation is a tactic of the enemy that he uses to keep us distanced from the love of God. We build walls between our sin and His mercy feeling as though we are undeserving, while the devil keeps handing us another brick to build higher and higher. If you allow him to convince you long enough that you are unable to be used by God, you'll eventually accept that lie too. So many wasted days of mine were spent believing that changing the nations and touching lives were for the superior Christians, the ones who walked hand in hand with Jesus on a daily basis.

Have you ever been there too? Have you looked at other Christian women, the ones who write all the books, conduct the conferences, manage the successful blogs, hold the microphone leading worship, and believe beyond a shadow of doubt that Jesus must do a standing ovation for them when they step into the building? You've thrown a smug look at them and thought, *God must prize you pretty highly to have used you in such significant ways. What do you do that I don't do?* Then you recall how you lost your temper or lied to your friend, fought with your husband, or unleashed on your children. You gossiped, swore, flipped out, and haven't opened your Bible in weeks, maybe months, and you have not darkened the doorstep of a church since your parents dragged you to Sunday school. I get it. I am her too.

There are days I still find myself summing and judging my sinful nature and disproportionately measuring it to my ability to be an effective tool for God's kingdom. If I am such a bad Christian, how will He ever let me lead others to Him? How is this mess of a woman able to or justified to be called as an ambassador for God? You can imagine, being the extremist I am, I went a bit overboard in the opposite direction. Suddenly, I swore to myself I would become "that" Christian—one step before joining a convent. You know, the apparently sinless one who does the Miss America wave when walking down the aisles of church.

I ran a super tight ship while being a gold star Christian. I never once cussed, maintained my temper, and never one time judged another, and my light shined brightly. How glorious that time was. I felt so incredibly proud of myself that I had finally achieved being the woman who I thought was pleasing to God. What amazing, rewarding, twenty-two seconds those were.

Come on, girl. Did you think I really reached the pinnacle of being without misdeed? I had you going there for a moment, though, didn't I? Being a sinful Christian doesn't make you any less of one; it makes you a real one. After years of frustration and heartache, I finally came to the realization that it has absolutely nothing to do with myself, but in everything to do with Who He is. I am who I am, because He is the great I Am.

Get this in your mind, woman. Jesus does not think you are a bad Christian. He knows you are flawed. He knew you would be before you took your first breath of life in this fallen world. That's why He came to die for you and me. We needed Him. It is you and me who put the constructs of measuring our success and levels of Christianity at an unattainable high; therefore, we actually distance ourselves from enjoying the inheritance of what being a Christian actually has to offer. We feel as though we must be religious machines without stain, and we suck the breath out of the abundant life God richly paid for to give us.

I have been working with children for over half a decade. Quite frankly, I have now met so many children that I admittedly have forgotten a good portion of them, not because they were any less special to me but simply because of the vast quantity that I've had the opportunity to serve. In the summer of 2015, I began working for another program within my agency, rather against my will to be honest. It was within this program that I worked with dozens of at-risk youth, and I spent a great deal of my time with them. Every chance I get within my job, I try to sow a seed of curiosity for Jesus within the kids. I don't teach the kids Bible verses. I don't ask them if they'd like to pray, nothing like that. I find it much more natural to wait for candid opportunities to shed light on His love. This may surface through general conversations such as what the Bible verses on my many bracelets that I wear mean or simply having K-Love on in my car so often that they end up memorizing the song lyrics. Anyway, one evening I was driving a group of kids home after the program, and one young man, roughly thirteen years old, asked me to change the station I had on because it was, in his opinion, rather boring. I struck up a conversation with him asking what kind of music was appealing to him, and as many preteen young men may suggest, he answered "rap."

This gave me an idea. I whipped my phone out at the next red light and quickly scrolled through my Pandora app to the Trip Lee radio station. If you don't know who Tripp Lee is and you don't mind rap, I recommend that be your next jam sesh, especially if you need a motivator to perform physical activity. The music began, and I watched his curious mind wonder why I was agreeing to play rap music, after I had insisted time again that it was typically inappropriate for young ears. I handed him my cell phone and smiled. "This is Christian music too."

I will never forget the look on that young man's face as he held my phone in amazement tossing his head back and forth enjoying the beat of the song. Oh, the joy it brought me to bring a stubborn, tough, though sweet teenage boy to rock on to the gospel. If I would have had a lighter, I would have probably started swaying my body and waving it back and forth. And although I was most satisfied that he was hearing the gospel of Jesus through his favored genre, I was also happy to see him having fun while doing so.

Listen to me. And please do not take this so literal that you become tempted to form an alliance of an angry mob declaring that every copy of this book be burned. I love Jesus. I love Him so much that there are truly no sum of words in *Webster's Dictionary* to convey my heart's passion for Him. I wake up daily and attempt to be the Christian woman whom I've learned from His Word He values. I live my life by a set of biblical standards, and I aspire to always let the world look to me and say, "She's a Christian, and boy oh boy, does she love her Jesus," even though I know I fail Him daily. Can someone say hallelujah? However, I also like to have fun. Yes, fun. Can you believe that the words Christian and fun can coexist in the same sentence? Hang tight before you call your pastor.

There is such a stigma associated with Christianity that you must endure life with the expectation of sainthood. That's why I shared the story about the young man who could not believe rappers exist who drop beats about the cross. People believe that Christians are boring and draining, with hands constantly folded in a prayer motion. Anything other than Christian music is sinful. Having a glass of wine at dinner with your friend, sister, or husband, well, you're a drunkard. Going to a country music concert with your girls and letting your hair down a little, oh, how dare you, you Jezebel. Now, again, before you become blushed thinking I am a lukewarm Christian and everything you have read thus far has been discredited, let me continue to validate myself.

Jesus wants you to enjoy life, sis. We as Christians, gifted with the salvation of eternal life, should have every reason known to mankind to be smiling from ear to ear. Sure, not every day looks that way. Trust me mine doesn't either. But we've created a reputation for ourselves that we do not know how to enjoy the life that God has blessed us with. I want that for you. I want that for myself too. I would often be driving for long periods of time in my car with my worship music playing, though feeling too guilty to check out my Brantley Gilbert Pandora country station. That's religion and law, my friends, not freedom. I highly doubt that Jesus is looking down on me with disappointment if I want to sing about some dirt roads and cowgirl boots. Jesus loves Brantley too, you know.

In the Word of God, Ecclesiastes 3:1–4 (NIV) reads, "For everything there is a season, and a time for every matter under Heaven…a time to weep, and a time to laugh; a time to mourn, and a time to dance." It is absolutely acceptable, rather encouraged, to have some fun. The Bible tells you so, you see? To laugh, sing, dance, and enjoy life. Now that is not, let me make that clear, *not*, a hall pass to go and do whatever you fancy that does not fall in line with our biblical principles. I am not at all encouraging you to go and sow your wild oats. Nor do I believe it is permissible to find the gray area in the black-and-white context of the Word of God. So don't put that on me, honey. The point is some of the most miserable people I have met in my life are Christians, not in the least bit because of Jesus but because of their own slavery. These people become religious androids that believe life should be consisted of living inside churches, constantly being oh-so-serious, or looking upon everything that is not associated with religion as a product straight from hell. It is as though these religious apparatuses believe that it is sinful to enjoy life. News flash, girlfriend: Jesus came so that we might have life and have it *abundantly* (John 10:10 NIV, emphasis mine). Jesus hung out with his friends, the disciples. Jesus attended the wedding feast, and might I add, He turned water into wine while attending. And I am willing to bet that during that wedding celebration, Jesus did not sit in the back at table number 24 with a frown on his face looking in disdain at those dancing in celebration. So often we become so focused on being the perfect, faultless Christians to attain God's love when all the while, while we were still sinners, Christ died for us (Romans 5:8 NIV). You are working for love and approval that has been established long before you even knew Who Jesus was. You are not a sorry excuse for a Christian. Nor are you a wasteful, too-far-gone sinful being who must earn brownie points to wear your faith badge proudly. Jesus's love is incessant. He is irrationally and irrevocably in love with you, and nothing and no one can stop His avid pursuit for your heart. You had nothing to do with gaining that love; it was already existing before the beginning of time. There is no height nor depth, no dark shadow of the earth you can hide where He will not reach His hand out toward you and offer you grace. Rather than hold your sin captive over your own head, I beg you to come to this realization. You are not big enough, bad enough, or sinful enough for Him to stop loving you. So stop telling yourself the opposite. He loved you first, and He loved you longest. More importantly, need you be reminded, you are forgiven, sis.

Stop, right now. Before you even continue that thought in your mind and tell yourself that I do not know what you've done, you are forgiven. I remember innumerable eye rolls I served reading about others speaking of their sins, making their bold confession about how they told a white lie to someone in their book club. Not making light of others' sin, but I would think to myself, *What about the big sins I've done, though?* Sin is sin. Christ died for the murderer as much as the gossiper. But in case you need to be reminded, you are as much forgiven for your unrighteous angry outburst as you were for the adultery, abortion, and the rest of the mind-shaking things you've been guilty of. He covered it all, every bit of it, and it's now unfounded under the blood. All of your un-qualifications, failed attempts at perfection, good, bad, and everything in between are nestled tightly under the umbrella of God's mercy.

It doesn't matter how many times you messed up, how many times you threw Jesus out of a window, or if you have your name etched in a hymn book on the back of a pew. Refuse to believe the lies from the enemy, and from your own self, that you are not Christian enough to be loved by Christ. Whatever your deficit, the cross paid in full.

Things to remember:

- Jesus saved you long before you even knew you needed saving and without your request.
- You don't have to wear a cape to be a part of Jesus's squad.
- When the enemy convinces you that you aren't worthy, remind him that he is worthless.
- Enjoy the life you have been given, in a godly fashion. It was purchased with a high price.
- Failure does not make you a bad Christian; it makes you a human dependent on a mighty Savior.

After reading this chapter:

Something that stuck with me is…

_____
_____
_____
_____
_____

Something I want to challenge myself with…

_____
_____
_____
_____
_____

This is how I am going to do it…

_____
_____
_____
_____
_____

My I Am Her statement is…

_____
_____
_____
_____
_____

CHAPTER 3
The Social Media Victim

Each one should test their own actions. Then they can take pride in themselves alone, without comparing themselves to someone else...
—Galatians 6:4 (NIV)

The grass isn't greener, they're just using a filter.
—Unknown

You feel the cold steel through your jeans as you're seated on the gymnasium bleachers. It's crowded, and there are women just like yourself seated all around you. You appear to be looking at each other trying to make sense of what the gathering is for. Some look anxious, others are perplexed, and the rest are perhaps rather disgruntled due to the confusion. Once asked, though, you plunge your arm up into the air in agreement that you too have been personally victimized by Regina George.

All right, I'm just building the momentum. This is not the script for the film *Mean Girls*. Quite honestly, due to the nature of that film, I question the popularity of that movie. However, that's how I feel about social media—personally victimized by it.

Now before you assume you know exactly where I am going with this chapter, let's have a quick powwow. Social media is a major millennial issue. I know that, you know that, and the prime minister of England knows that. We know the what, but do we really understand the *why*? If I took a poll of everyone reading this book and asked them whether or not they believed that social media portrayed negative viewpoints or victimized others into feelings of inadequacy or comparison, most of you would agree that that statement does in fact have validity. I want to get deep, though—nitty-gritty, dirt on your forehead, beads of sweat dripping deep into this hot topic. Trust me we have enough material to do so. I'm just placing my bets now that social media is going to become a college major at some university before we know it. In fact, it may even already be instated. I've seen the studies of the algorithm for gaining followers; and, guys, this is some next-level calculus. So let's dig in.

May I begin by just confessing the countless hours I have spent on social media stalking one incredible female public figure to the next and the next and then the next after that? Hundreds of thousands of followers, tens of thousands of likes, breathtaking house, coiffed husband, polished children, striking wardrobes—I could go on and on and on. I mean some gals just have it all, right? *How did they get there?* I would often wonder. What did she do so differently in her life than I did or didn't do? Amid one of my plaintive pouts one afternoon, I put my phone down and resurfaced from the pit of social media doom I was spiraling in. Social media depression is a real thing, guys. I will fight you on that any day of the week. But before we continue to touch on that, I have some mind-boggling questions if you'll just entertain me briefly. Let me just ask something. Maybe someone can help me out here with this ever so burning question surfing throughout my mind. How do women get these gorgeous, professional-looking photographs on a daily basis? I mean, do they have tripods? No, wait! Perhaps they have a little entourage they've hired with a background in professional photography that captures their small moments throughout the day. Of course they import those images into Photoshop and make sure the brightness and exposure are nothing less than superb, all building up to that moment of tapping "Share." I also wonder, though, who on this big, blue, and green orbiting planet feels the need to document the most mundane tasks of life and share them on the internet for millions of viewers to see? I don't know about you; but I would genuinely feel awkward asking a friend, family member, or innocent bystander to snap a photo of me in the middle of TJ Maxx holding my latest and greatest finds—props to you gals who are always camera ready to capture your daily activities. As for me, no one wants to see me pushing my cart through Target because half of the time I don't even know where I am going. It's not cute, it's not sharable, and I look lost. Sad to say, even candid photographs are now posed. Oh, and I'm guilty of it too. I won't lie to you. You know when you are posing for a picture and happen to laugh so hard at something that wasn't even funny? Of course you appear to have just chuckled like a hyena so your photograph looks like you were having an experience of a lifetime. I once attempted doing that with my sister, and we laughed hysterically the entire time. And even those pictures did not produce naturally fun images. I looked barbaric. I did not even know what to do with my body. Ladies, please, help me out here. Where do you place your hands? I never know what to do with them if I am taking a photo el solo. I awkwardly stand there like I'm stiff. All right, back on track now. End rant.

One of our greatest social media issues is that we have become entirely way too obsessed with recording a moment that we have forgotten how to genuinely have it. We need some help, guys, desperately. First of all, let us bust this notion that life is perfectly able to be documented at all times. Convince yourself all that you want and break out the streamers for your little pity party about how much better off everyone is than you are, but think about it. No one is going to share with the world what they look like in the morning, the fight they had with their husband the night before, their children's colossal mistakes, or that nasty old t-shirt that's the most frequent article of clothing on their body. It just does not happen that way. But that's where social media depression is birthed. I would love to show you my camera roll every time I try to take a selfie. There are about forty-seven headshots of what appears to be the same exact face; but when I scan through them for review, you hear "Nope, nope, nope, oh what-the-double-chin nope." I'm not going to post those ones. They get deleted. And then I affirm they've been permanently removed out of my "Deleted" album. I don't want everyone to see that version of me or my life. None of us share those unsharable moments. Rather, we brag about the accomplishments and embellish our lifestyles to impress everyone around us. We want people to window-shop our lives. Whether we do it subconsciously or not, we are in a constant match trying to get ahead of everyone else around us. But why? When did we get so competitive among each other?

Years ago, no one knew what you were doing. Granted, your close circle of family, friends, and whoever else you let knew your private business, was primarily shared via the telephone through calls and eventually text messages. We did not have the outlets to social media at the tap of a phone icon. Do you remember when you accidentally hit the up arrow on your cell phone and the internet would pop up? You nearly threw your phone in some toilet water and acted as though it was a hand grenade. Ah, those were the good old days.

My generation was the ever so fortunate one to be introduced to social media. I remember everyone in junior high school raving about this thing called MySpace. Did I just shove anyone on a jaunt down memory lane? This personal webpage was just the chipping block of the social media introductory for myself which generated a lot of hurt in my youth. I remember my fellow peers spending countless hours personalizing their pages. You could add music, create a background, and of course update your photos and post endless amounts of them. What I remember most about MySpace, though, was that you had a "Top Friends" section. Here, you would rank your friends in order, typically ranging from one through eight. That in itself was drama overload. What do you think young, teenage girls did when they got into quarrels? Well, my dear, you got bumped down from the top eight list; sometimes ya got booted right off the page. I want to know who is responsible for coming up with the idea that people should put others in a ranking order, and then broadcast it on the internet. It's madness. Not only does it not make sense or seem completely idiotic; it's just simply mean. MySpace coincided with AIM (instant messaging if you are a tad younger than myself), which was a quick way to notify the majority that someone kissed the boy you liked or one girl was mad at another, and of course some vicious cyberbullying took place here. Moving forward, MySpace paved the way for Facebook, Facebook to Twitter, and Twitter to Instagram; and then the ever so shady Snapchat flashed us with its charming feature of deleting pictures sent or received within ten seconds or less. I mean we were set up for failure, people. I almost feel bad for us. Almost. But now we have this giant, ugly, cyber mess on our hands. We can either not succumb to the social media masses and dare to refrain from that world altogether (which may be rather dramatic) or, as most of us do, take on the philosophy "if you can't beat 'em, join 'em." So here we are, like being sucked into the East Australian Current. We are tossed in a whirlwind of cyber madness, which brings me to the *why*.

Why is social media such a heavy-weighted, complex subject we find ourselves so warped with? If the mission of social media is to connect, network, and share with others, why are we having such a problem with it? While writing this chapter, I sat down and took out a scrap sheet of paper in efforts to trigger some quick response emotions from my brain. I picked up a pen and ferociously wrote the first five feelings I elicited from visualizing the words "social media." Here is what I came up with, and mind you, it took me less than ten seconds to do this: Insecure. Insignificant. Inadequate. Small. Covet.

Those were the first five words that easily rolled off my tongue, or pen in this case, when reflecting on how social media made me feel. Now I'm sure you understand what those words mean and you don't need a vocabulary lesson, but I want to explain to you how my brain chose those words out of the dictionary pool.

I was insecure that my social media game was flat-out weak. I did not have a lot of followers, I maxed out at about 130 likes, and I hardly had people engaging in my posts. Can we say #boring? I felt insignificant to the other ladies I followed who had just the opposite of me. You know the ones you have to stop for a bathroom break while scrolling through their copious pages of comments on their latest selfie? Those ones. I wasn't important enough for someone to take out the time for me as they did for them. Inadequacy surfaced easily when I saw that even when I tried to gain momentum, when I tried to produce growth on my account, I spun my tires in soupy mud. I was small, no one knew about me, and 99 percent of those who did simply did not care. And forget about having the need to have a fancy little blue checkmark by my name—totally unnecessary in my case. Yet what caused the most grief to my mental well-being was the nasty temptation of comparison. I coveted everything "she" had that I didn't.

I'm going to ask you to do some honest thinking here and answer a few questions for yourself before we continue. Consider it your very own social media composition exercise. What I want to do is examine the trends that have formed throughout the evolution of social media. Be truthful. You're the only one who is going to know the responses anyway. Here we go:

1. Have you ever shared someone else's post with a close friend or family member to make fun of someone or judge them negatively, even if it was just between the two of you?
2. Have you ever chosen an outfit you've planned on wearing due to the excitement of sharing it on social media for people to see what you have on?
3. Have you ever been excited for an experience solely to then be able to share it on social media?
4. Do you plan extensively in your mind how you are going to share big news or an exciting event?
5. Have you ever gone to a concert, sporting event, party, or any other social gathering and posted pictures on social media before the event was over?
6. Have you ever been saddened by the posts of others feeling that their lives appear much better than yours?
7. Do you feel as though you have to measure up by showing your milestones in life to others such as engagements, weddings, pregnancies, graduations, and careers or reaching other goals?
8. Have you developed patterns of "checking" on certain people's pages consistently to keep track of what they are up to?
9. How many social media accounts do you have?
10. How many times have you checked those just today?

Now, before you feel vexed or even embarrassed for answering a lot of those questions with "yes," please don't feel shamefaced, for

I will unashamedly confess to you that I have a solid "yes" after each of those questions. Hello, I am her. Remember? We've all been guilty of at least a few of those statements, if not all. Yet when it's presented this way, it makes us seem rather piteous, doesn't it? As I scan through those questions, I speculate just how much social media infiltrates my life. However, I didn't ask you to take the "quiz of shame" to make you feel pathetic. Rather, I want to enlighten you how this phenomenon and the hierarchy of others' approval is controlling not just your life, but your outlook on it as well.

We are slowly turning into zombies and won't even pause to recognize it. That device that never rests less than two feet away from us controls most of what we say, think, or do. I mean we now feel compelled to take a picture of our food, hungry as a horse, but by golly you don't pick up that nugget until you showed the world that you ate at Chick-fil-A today. We are oversharing everything, and the more we share, the more we feel the need to keep up with everyone on our following list. And whether we'd like to admit it or not, 99.9 percent of the time we post, we do it for one of two reasons: to convince people, even ourselves, of our seemingly wonderful lives or to brag about them. The other .1 percent of the people sharing either have a healthy balance of maintaining social media or use it for its intended purpose—to connect with each other. Let me break this down even more. We strive to demonstrate a constructed reality that we really don't live to impress people whom we really don't like. You spend more time taking a picture of the flowers your husband just sent you in order to post them than actually bending down to smell them. So do you want to actually enjoy a bountiful life or waste time documenting that you have one? Mhm, am I reaching anyone yet?

I know I may come off a bit harsh during this discussion, but I want us all to have a wake-up call. As I continue to see the trends among ourselves channeling through our Facebooks and Instagrams, I'm beginning to understand why we've succumbed to this point. Let's bust a few myths about Madam Social Media.

First, you are doing enough, you have enough, and you *are* enough.

There's something about this enthusiasm of stalking each other's lives that makes you feel like you ought to be a master at multiple things. We millennials take it to a whole new level of edifying our-selves and proving our craftwork to each other. Might I add, I have never seen so many self-made businesses sprung forth. With each tap on the Instagram icon on my iPhone, I swear another person who bought a DSM camera is now a photographer. Don't get me wrong. I support any person to pursue their passions and follow their dreams. Remember I encourage you to do so wholeheartedly. I also promote small-town folk dreaming big. C'mon. I'm that girl myself! Yet somehow chasing dreams has turned into chasing credibility. I have friends and acquaintances who have upcycled furniture, made custom cookies, personalized wreaths, and became party planners out of thin air. Let's also not forget the videographers, life coaches, fitness coaches, shake drinkers, t-shirt makers, and at-home entrepre-neurs. Did I miss any? Becoming any of those things is wonderful, and I would proudly be your first customer, though what itches me is, would we still pursue those passions if we couldn't post about them? Are we doing these things more for ourselves, or are we forcing busyness to exemplify success?

We are constantly faced with people on our friends list who are achieving one accomplishment after the next and adding more letters after their name that if you are simply working a nine-to-five or staying at home to raise your babies, you just cannot hang. You have no contribution to this big bad world. Or everyone else your age is married by now and having babies or adopting at least one child from Uganda, but you and your boyfriend just broke up so you are back at square one. You are falling so behind and nowhere near the leaderboard. In fact, you are not only not on the same page as them. You're not even in the same chapter as they are, maybe not even in the same book.

That. Is. Nonsense! If you want to become the CEO of the business in your own living room, girl, I will stand up and slow clap for you. I will cheer you on, and I vow to be one of the purchasers of your product. But if you are trying to find a niche to fit in with everyone else on your feed, please, just stop. You are enough. What you do in a day's work is enough. And everything you have is enough. You might follow someone with an island containing accessories in her closet, but you hardly have enough clothes to fill your five-foot sliding door one. That's not what measures *true* success in this life. You do the best you can with what you've got, and God will handle the rest. Relax.

Second, don't compete; appreciate.

We need to stop hating on the talent that she #1 has or the gift she #2 possesses or the knacks that she #3 has mastered. News flash, girl: You cannot slay at everything. No one is good at the whole shebang; that's why we need each other. Indulge with me, for one moment here. What if instead we took off our stank faces and bad attitudes toward our neighbors and alternatively worked together to achieve something for the greater good? I'm not talking about necessarily physically getting together and building a giant Lego house. I mean, if a girl you know put her heart into a fashion blog and looks like Jenny from the block in her photo, tell her that. If some girl you know is posting fifteen videos a day of her workout and it annoys you, let her be; it makes her feel good about herself. And if this one loves posting makeup tutorials and someone else is trying to sell their hair products and that one created a webpage, would it be utterly detrimental to your health to encourage them? Guys, we need to support each other. It's crucial to building a community of strong, supporting women and essential to promoting a catalyst for change from what we've been experiencing.

I learned a teeny lesson from a little, tiny birdy one day that I hadn't intended on hypothesizing. My mother and I were in a large parking lot feeding geese and birds that were overpopulating the area. We noticed there was no disposed food lying around, and my caring mother who loves to feed anyone or anything searched through the car for some crackers. We watched together as the birds rowdily scurried to the broken bits of food we casted out. This one little sassy guy caught my eye, though, and I focused on his behavior the rest of our time spent there. There was food all around him, literally bits of cracker droppings surrounding his two tiny clawed feet. Instead of casually munching on all that was around him, he gazed at the birds next to him eating. After some time, he eventually approached the other birds and fought them for the food they were preying on. I'll tell you I've never seen birds fight, but this was team serious, guys. Without overthinking and before turning this visual into a deep well-thought-out lesson, I said aloud, "Ma, look at that little guy. He is more concerned with the food the other birds have than all the food lying around at his feet." She turned her head toward me and said, "Well, now that's just a whole sermon in itself."

Let the little rambunctious guy teach you too. Stop obsessing over everyone else enjoying their crackers while not appreciating your own. You know that I do not literally mean crackers. I am speaking about your career, your marriage, your children, your passions, your clothes, your hair, and everything that motivates you to express that you are keeping in cahoots with everyone around you. There are women who do things that you cannot, and there are others who could never do what you do. We all contribute in some way or another in the arena of life. So stop competin' and start appreciatin'.

Third, sharing is not always caring.

The world doesn't have to know if I am on cloud nine or in the trenches. No one needs to know that I made a new pot roast recipe last night for dinner and everyone who ate it loved it. I do not have to share photos of my Christmas decor while knowing about five out of the nine hundred friends who follow me will actually be at my home. I can have those things, live that life, and most importantly enjoy it, without anyone knowing. Have you ever heard the philosophical statement "If a tree falls in the woods with no one there, does it really make a sound?" Well, if it's not posted on social media, did it still happen? My point is our private lives were never intended to be a public service announcement. You will enjoy more moments as they occur than all the wasted ones being worried about documenting them. Don't just post about leaving a basket of goodies for the Amazon truck driver at your front door; greet him yourself and thank him. Be the person who you post that you are.

Now before we get carried away, I'm not a Facebook hater or Instagram slammer (hey, that has a nice ring to it). I too can be found on social media, and I encourage you to join my community. You will find that I enjoy posting an occasional forty-some-time attempted selfie or hilarious quote I found on Pinterest to share with my followers.

So I am not at all suggesting that we light torches and stand outside of Mark Zuckerberg's home demanding restitution for this phenomenon we've become entrapped with. Nor should you close this book and delete all of your social media accounts in the name of justice. The difference is I stopped letting it control how I did things in my life and simply utilized it for what it is: a fun accessory. I use it to connect and to share encouragement, laughter, and Jesus with others. I worry now not about impressing my followers or friends or some random stranger who lands on my feed and instead about impressing God and myself. That's it. As for the rest of my followers, well, you'll just have to use your imagination and guess what I ate for breakfast today.

So here's my challenge to you, which you may or may not accept. I know reading this book thus far has been exhausting with all of my requests. There's no pressure, though I'm interested to see how reconnected you feel to God, your family, friends, and yourself should you choose to engage. For the next week, be it shorter or longer if you'd like, remain offline. Unplug, girl. Did you just panic a little bit even thinking of this dare? If social media is a part of your business, by all means do what you got to do. But if it's just freed time you waste throughout your day, disengage for a week. Stop and smell the roses—literally. Don't post, do not tweet, do not scroll through countless photos that everyone is posting, and simply exist without anyone but your closest gang knowing what you are doing. Read. Journal. Cook. Go for a walk in the park. In fact, download a Bible app on your smartphone; and every time you feel compelled to pick up your phone to sign on to social media, and you will notice just how many times in a day you do this, read a few Bible verses instead.

I promise you we are all in this thing together. We may all be at different stages, but this truth resonates within each of us. So the next time you are peeling through all the news feeds, though I do encourage you to give yourself a break from them, pause and remember: We all have bad days; we all have our issues. We all have ugly selfies, and we all started with zero followers. Every one of us has struggles that are hidden in the darkest corners of our hearts and homes. Just as well, every one of us has our victories and successes. You might be seeing her epic production now, but you never saw all of her rehearsals. So do not be discouraged by someone else's crowning moments. You don't know how hard she worked to get there, and likewise for yourself. In a world full of Gretchen Wieners and Regina Georges, be different. Support her, applaud her, and, more than anything, do not envy her. Do not feel so compelled that you need to convince people you have a life worth viewing; just live it. And sometimes, you just have to be #signedout.

Things to remember:

- It doesn't matter what everyone thinks about you, because truthfully, all that matters is what you know about you.
- Social media in itself is not necessarily evil; it's how we use it that makes it socially dangerous.
- None of our lives are perfect, regardless of what our Instagram feed suggests.
- You control social media; it does not control you. (So don't let it.)
- Disengage from the race of life. You're going at your own pace, and that's perfectly fine.

After reading this chapter:

Something that stuck with me is…

_____

_____

_____

_____

_____

Something I want to challenge myself with…

_____

_____

_____

_____

_____

This is how I am going to do it...

_____

_____

_____

_____

_____

My I Am Her statement is...

_____

_____

_____

_____

_____

CHAPTER 4
The Divorcee

Never will I leave you; never will I forsake you.
—Hebrews 13:5 (NIV)

Forget what hurt you but never forget what it taught you.
—Shannon L. Alder

*In three words I can sum up everything I've
learned about life: it goes on.*
—Robert Frost

I am currently going through a div—Wait. Let me try that again.
I wasn't ready. My husband of four months of marriage and I are
getting divorc—

D-I-V-O-R-C-E. Divorce.

You could presume I just entered a second grade spelling bee
and received a word I had never heard of. I literally choked on it as it
exited my mouth. Somehow, that word did not belong in my vocabulary. Even when it became time to sound out those syllables, they
couldn't, or maybe just wouldn't, roll off of my tongue.

If you would have asked me years ago if I had thought divorce
would ever be in my agenda, I would have probably laughed you out
of my presence. It was never in my plans, never in my picket fence
portrait, and certainly not something that I imagined would happen
so prematurely. It was not because I dubbed myself too good for
divorce, but I committed myself to never coming to that decision,

no matter how hard or how ugly my marriage would have gotten. Never. Yet there I was, twenty-seven years old as a four-month-and-some-week-long newlywed, driving back to my mother's house after my former husband told me he had "checked out" of our marriage.

I got into my car that evening, a duffle bag as my passenger, my four-pound dog on my lap; and as I reversed out of my driveway, I turned to stare at my house knowing it would never look the same again. That house symbolized the newest, most exciting chapter of my life—my home, a place I dreamt of returning to with my new-born babies in the backseat. The flower bed of hydrangeas suddenly resembled weeds, welcome home turned into strangeness, and what I believed to be the host of many memories and milestones to come now became a plagued box of painful, empty walls.

I had convinced myself for mornings that followed that evening that it was all just a foggy nightmare and soon I would be awakening and snap out of this misery. You know that moment when you first arise roughly two seconds before you swipe the crust from your eye-lids when reality starts setting in? It's like little, tiny pebbles of real life pelting you in the face. *Pew. Pew.* I could have hidden under the covers and avoided the sunlight at all costs, but the truth each and every morning was that "He is gone, you are getting divorced, and wait a second. Is this *still* really happening?" It was a new actuality I was forced to come to terms with. I could not stop him from leaving. I could not press pause or alter the course of events taking place. I could not change the fact that my dream home was now tainted with a For Sale sign in the front yard. I could not freeze all of the fast-paced occurrences that were swarming around me like flies. I felt powerless, defeated, desperate, and overwhelmingly hopeless. I wanted to lie in my defeat and set up camp there and maybe get a nice little sign to hang outside of my tent that read "I give up," wave a beaten, rugged white flag, and throw a few prickly cacti around to really set the tone of the drab environment. Homey, huh?

It is incredibly true that you go through stages of emotions during hardships. Mine were as follows: shock, sadness, disbelief, anger, depression, denial, and then acceptance (sort of). Everyone has their own patterns of dealing with difficult times, and if you expect yourself to fit into some preset mold, save your energy. While there are patterns and similarities found among people going through identical situations, we are all different, and we tend to heal our emotions in various ways. I tried to fit into this construct that I should now be moving toward the next phase, and if I was in the acceptance phase, why was I still sad or angry? You feel the way you feel, and you cannot change that. A spiritual father of mine has always reminded me, "Feelings are real. They can be wrong, but they are real." And he's right. It's how you manage them that's important, though. I will be honest with you. There were days in the anger phase where I would have loved to binge a "telling off the world" campaign with some not-so-friendly vocabulary. I couldn't help that feeling; it was real to me and I was hurting.

The day when I felt most angry, though, was the day I was served with my divorce papers. That anger was almost tangible. It wasn't reading through the decree, or even the fact that I held them in my hands now, though that did rip me to pieces. When I turned to the last page and saw my then husband's signature on that black line, I not only felt my heart begin to physically cry but also I became enraged. What that signature represented was "Yes, this is what I consent to, dissolution of marriage." I began to experience every stage I previously spoke of in the matter of moments. I cried, screamed, found myself in denial again that I would be signing divorce papers, and eventually had to walk outside to fill my lungs with fresh air before I imploded.

After pulling myself together, I had to return back to real life again. Fun as it may be to stay in that moment, we're big girls now, right? We cannot dwell in our state of pity, throw a tantrum, and always get our way. That's for the terrible two crew. But oh, if only it were as easy as eating a Happy Meal to fix everything. It's not, though, albeit it may help just a little bit. This new life felt strange, fearful, and undesirable to say the least. But it was here, and it was beckoning for me whether I wanted to step into it or not.

It took about twenty-four hours before people outside of my close-knit pack would learn of my husband leaving. One person told another, and then they told a few more; and before I even realized, half of the town knew within days. It became old news before I had even begun to process it myself. My house went on the market within days and was publicized online by the real estate agency for the general public to view. To this day, I never once viewed my home for sale online. I felt exposed, as if I was naked in downtown square for everyone to see. My customized, decorated home was now being toured by realtors and buyers and viewed by all the nosy inquirers in town. I walked in a room, and people looked at me like a wounded dog on a Sarah McLachlan commercial. I would sit on the floor in my house as it emptied and watched strangers coming in to purchase my furniture and walk out the door with it. A small piece of me left with them each time. I wanted to scream at the top of my lungs and spend the next few months on an island far away from town where everyone knew my name. People who came into my home would often find me in a corner in tears, and I still felt humiliated of the situation I was left to deal with. I grew more and more numb amid the months of appropriating financial decisions and legal matters. I was on a rampage of emotions. I even found myself playing God with my ex-husband. I chased and sought. I pleaded and grew so frustrated that he wouldn't acknowledge the weight of his decision. But then I remembered we are called to be *like* Christ, not be Christ. Whether it was as evident as a blimp in the sky or as minuscule as a grain of sand on the ocean floor, his choices were no longer my concern. I could not save my husband nor myself for that matter of sin; only Jesus could. So I tucked it in, put it to rest, and gave it to God where it belonged.

Before we carry on, I want to mark a giant exclamation point encompassing the meat of this chapter. What it's not is a mantra to my estranged ex-husband. Regardless of the circumstances involving our termination of marriage, I wish him well. This chapter is also not a sappy pity story walking through the sorrows of my divorce. I don't want to relive it, and I'm more than sure you don't care much to read about it. This isn't about why I got divorced or a documentary of the occasion. What this chapter is, however, is not only a hand holding for my fellow divorcees but also a reminder that God turns your bitter into better.

So if you have found yourself, as I did, forced to face the reality of being labeled with the big ol' "D" on your forehead, let me reassure you of a few things. First, it really, truly is going to be okay. You are going to hear that about 792 times, but it's the truth. So trust me on that. This is not going to stick with you, this will not define you, and it does not mean you were or are a bad wife. It's simply just another chapter in your story. For the duration of my divorce process, I considered myself as a bad spouse. Truthfully, I am surprised I didn't literally wear a scarlet letter "D" on my clothing because I felt so shameful—shameful that my marriage failed and everyone around me my age was still married and embarrassed that people must be thinking I had to be a terrible wife in order to be abandoned so quickly. You name it. I thought it. Through all the negative self-talk, I had to remind myself that what happened to me was not a reflection of who I really was. Was I a perfect wife? Absolutely not. They don't exist. I have not met one on this side of the Mississippi, so if you know of her, please do send my heartfelt condolences.

Now, next and most important, you are not eternally shunned out of God's grace. I do not know if you were the wronged or did the wrong, nor do I know the circumstances of your divorce. However, I can assure you that you have not fallen too far out of the love of God. It absolutely pains me that Christians are too busy judging their divorced brothers and sisters rather than supporting them through this difficult time. Oh and news flash: Jesus's bloodline descended from King David, an adulterer, and Jesus was the first and only to extend His hand toward the woman caught in the very act of adultery and offer her grace. Can we say mercy?

Lastly, he may have left you or perhaps even betrayed you, but God did not. And He won't. I had this certain epiphany one afternoon while communing with a co-worker, which shifted my brain back into focus and gave me a little jolt that I needed to progress toward healing. After staring back at the twelfth person with shock on their face, I was newly presented with the question, "What are you going to do now? He was your life." I'm not sure if the perplexity on my face was physically obvious in a "what-the-what" type of complexion, but I felt it internally. There was a fine balance streaming through me of both disturbance and sadness that one would think another human being has that much impact on the value of their own life. I had loved my husband, but to say he *was* my life was a bit extreme. In that moment, I was able to not only reassure this concerned individual but more importantly remind myself that "Jesus Christ is my life; he's just a man." And men leave, but Jesus stays.

Let me rephrase that. Boys leave; Jesus stays.

Of those three woes of my divorce, the one I struggled with the most was using the divorce to put an invisible, though sturdy, fence in between God and me. I've always found myself to be one of those Christians who will tromp my hypothetical march with my burning torch chanting grace to all those around. I indulge myself with convincing people they are covered by the grace of God and nothing in their past, present, or future could separate them from the love of Christ. That grace applies to every single breathing human on this planet, but me. At least that's how I understood it. If I watched someone steal something in front of me and then found them hiding in a dark alley, I could easily approach and pour out warmth like smooth, melted butter yielding God's mercy and forgiveness. But if I myself did as much as slip a cuss word, oh, honey, I was thrown into exile out of God's family. As you can imagine then, following my divorce I was consumed with what it meant spiritually. If I had been presented with the concept of God forgiving someone who had gotten a divorce prior to my own, I would have been more perplexed at why you would even ask me such a preposterous question. After going through a divorce myself, though, I acted as if I was Erin Brockovich and preparing my case before God and all those around me.

I became obsessed, literally obsessed, with reading countless theologians and pastors' take on divorced peoples. Now, I am no theologian myself, nor am I your pastor; so I beg you not to credit me with a biblical standpoint on divorce. It's horrible, and God hates it, but He loves *you*. I do not condone divorce, and I would never, ever suggest nor encourage it as a viable option. Marriage is a sacred covenant made not only with man and wife but with God Almighty that should be taken as serious as until death do you part. But the sad reality is that Christians' divorce rate is as high as the rest of the population's, and it's something that we are often faced to deal with. If you are currently going through or previously have gone through a divorce and are struggling as I was, I encourage you to seek stable, biblically based, Christian counseling that would support you and lead you in the right direction. I am not the one to tell you whether your divorce was based on biblical grounds or not or pat your back saying you were the wronged party and justice shall seek you. Though I am not certified to do any of that, as a sister in Christ, I am able to assure you of this: Divorced people are no less in God's eyes, they are not failures or outcasts, and they are not the weak link in the chain of God's kinship. They are every bit as covered in grace and love in the eyes of our Father, as the man who hung on the cross next to Christ. Remind yourself of that, because I do daily. Now, remember when I said God is in the business of turning bitter to better? Here's how He turned my pain into purpose.

The last month of my marriage was for lack of better terms miserable. Each night I pulled into my driveway, I was filled with anxiety as to what I would be walking into. All I wanted to do was take all of the arguments we previously had and successfully place them in the past. For whatever reason, that just couldn't be done by one party. I begged—literally down on my knees begged. That's one regret among the many that I have. The only one you should ever fall on your knees for is Christ. However, I let myself succumb so lowly because I assumed that's what God wanted me to do—to belittle myself at all costs, just to ensure my marriage worked. I cannot tell you how to successfully navigate through a divorce. I made my own mistakes through it, and if you're forced to face divorce as well, I'm sure you will too. Though I made mistakes during that time, I also made some choices I am quite proud of too.

I thought God would wait for me to be through the storm for me to become useful. I assumed years later, once I had completely healed from the divorce, I would then be able to be affective and help others going through the same. That wasn't His plan, though. God began using me as soon as days after the separation by how people were noticing me. Whether I had felt it deep within or not, when I showed strength, when I showed my trust was in the Lord and that my dedication was still toward my husband until those papers were signed, it gave others hope and encouragement as well. I would remind them that God was in control of my marriage and whether my husband followed his will for divorce or God produced a miracle and we reconciled, I was content in either decision. I might have felt out of control, but I rested in knowing that He still was. In the meantime, I was able to encourage others as I healed. And in the midst of being comforted, I became the comforter. And that, my friends, is a true blessing.

What I learned during this season, what I hope for you to understand after reading this, is sometimes things are a part of God's will, even if they don't feel like they are. Just because something is difficult does not mean it's not a part of God's plan for your life. If you don't believe me, just look at the destiny in the cross. It's not to say that God willingly shoots cannonballs of hardships our way, but He wasn't surprised by my divorce. On the day of my wedding, God heard us commit our marriage vows to Him, yet He knew in that very moment of marital bliss where that matrimony would eventually lead. He did not jump off His throne in shock that evening and pace the floors of heaven in pandemonium. He knew it would happen, but He also knew how to use that horror to shape and mold me into the woman He knew I was destined to become. This season stripped me, broke me, and wrecked me to the core. Yet it also gifted me the opportunity to renovate. It enabled me to find myself, the real me, and allowed God to rebuild and birth purpose into my life. It enabled me to help you.

I learned never to settle for anything less than what I know I deserve. I also learned that despite what label others may attach to me, I refuse to live up to those expectations. During the difficult nights, the nights that I cried murmuring through a shaking voice and heavy tears, I saw no hope. *How*, I would wonder, *will God use this for something good? How will this be more than just a miserable experience?* This was a chapter of my story, some crinkled pages in my book, and one day of the year that will forever to me be tainted by an anniversary of a failed forever. I cannot change that. But it doesn't have to end there.

Leading up to my divorce, I was encouraged by a spiritual leader to create a very detailed list of what I would be looking for in a man in the future. He advised me to be extremely detailed with God, because after all, God is a God of even the smallest details. I liked the idea of this, but I committed to myself that I would not even entertain a list until I consented to my divorce papers. In my eyes, why dream of another man while I was still married to one, even though my current husband was in another state? The time eventually came when the secretary from the attorney's office called me and said, "The ninety days has expired, and your divorce papers are ready for your signature." My mother drove me to the office on that warm, summer day, and I had a t-shirt dress on that said "New Season." I had previously bought myself a necklace with a little blue butterfly on it to wear after I had signed my papers. For me, that symbolized me stepping into my newest season in life and reminded me that just like the caterpillar, a butterfly would evolve from this. And it did.

When I reflect upon that heartbroken, terrified girl on that cold February evening, I can no longer find her in my reflection. She defined her security in her circumstances and in a man and not her God. That girl measured her womanhood in being a wife and having the all-American family image. But that girl does not exist anymore. Now, I introduce myself to you as a new woman, a woman who knows her state, her stability, and an unfailing love that rests in Christ alone. It took losing "him," to truly find who I am in *Him*. It took his broken promises to rely on God's never-changing ones.

I viewed myself as I did the wilted, dead hydrangeas in my once beloved flower bed. I was listless, weighted down, and covered in dirt. I looked hopeless and less than desirable. However, God sowed and toiled the weeds away from my roots and planted me firmer than I stood before. And after some time, after the season shifted as they always do, my color returned and I glowed a bit brighter than I did before. There were some storm clouds that covered my sunshine at times undeniably. And believe me, if you are no stranger to this chapter in your own story, there is going to come a moment when after doing everything in your God-given power, you are going to have to let go too. But when you let go of all those expectations, all of the pain, and all of the hopes and dreams, you gain something in return. I'm not abandoned. I'm not divorced. I am not damaged goods, nor am I someone's discarded regret. I am not undeserving of love, and I am not a failure because of a previous marriage. None of those things define who I am. I am a daughter so loved by God that He couldn't stand to see something meant for harm not be used for my good. And so are you. Divorce isn't your story; it's just a chapter in your book.

Besides, at the end of one chapter, another one begins. Just flip the page.

Things to remember:

- Divorce may be a part of you, but it does not define you.
- Heal at your own pace. There is not a twelve-step program for a mending heart.
- There is no sin that can separate you from the grace of God; yes, that includes divorce.
- Do not allow the enemies' attack to gain more attention than God's resurrection of your situation.
- When you're forced to let go, that's when you have to let God.

After reading this chapter:

Something that stuck with me is…

_____

_____

_____

_____

_____

Something I want to challenge myself with…

_____

_____

_____

_____

_____

This is how I am going to do it...

_____

_____

_____

_____

_____

My I Am Her statement is...

_____

_____

_____

_____

_____

CHAPTER 5
The Perfectionist

But he said to me, "My grace is sufficient for you, for my power is made perfect in weakness." Therefore I will boast all the more gladly about my weaknesses, so that Christ's power may rest on me.
—2 Corinthians 12:9 (NIV)

I'm a recovering perfectionist and an aspiring "good-enoughist."
—Brene Brown

I believe I'm at the age where I am no longer a part of the cool generation. There are just some fads that I am catching onto way too late and find myself asking the younger crowd to educate me. I remember one evening I was skimming through my Instagram feed and a young fashion blogger was encouraging her followers to check out another blogger's free presets. Preset? Uhm, what? Thank the good Lord I am always one "Open new tab" away from Google.

Go to find out, need you be informed as well, presets are essentially saved filters in Lightroom (which I also learned is the newer, modern sister of Photoshop). Apparently this newest trend that I was oblivious to has taken over many Instagram accounts. When I was new to "the gram" many moons ago, I was intrigued with the various different filters as I curiously swiped my photo through a series of updated, more appealing versions of itself. However, we have now graduated from a window of Valencia or Clarendon to establishing presets so that all 1,304 of our photos match each other's lighting. Ugh, the pressure.

I assumed in order to have an appealing Instagram feed, I must jump on the preset bandwagon as well and construct a theme for myself. Side commentary: Can you believe what we consume our time with in this century? Get this, though. You can actually purchase presets on Etsy. Yes, there are people who make presets and allow you to purchase them for roughly five dollars to make your pictures more attractive and uniform in appearance. I won't lie. I had about three in my cart that I was debating with for a few days. I took the plunge, and I eventually bought one. That was a grueling challenge, by the way. I had to learn how to download these presets into the mobile version of Lightroom on my phone, which took me into the wee hours of the morning to finally apply. However, after all of my hard work, I did it for absolutely nothing. I canned the presets.

Now, I will never condone a person for using a filter. Girl, they make our pictures pretty. There's no denying that. While I encourage you to love every inch of your own skin and not doctor up your photos, we all do it sometimes; we all swipe the filters. I would be lying to you if I told you I have never used any. Yet the whole preset thing, well, it took things to a whole new level for me. We weren't just stopping at playing around with the color in pictures, but now making a consistent theme to culminate our feeds. So I took a stance, a millennial stance if you will, that no matter if I remain with a following list of three hundred or three hundred thousand, I would not utilize a preset. Go ahead and hold me to it. Did you just roll your eyes at me for this incredibly feeble pledge? Good, I would roll mine too. You know what it is, though? I am tired of perfectionism and striving to obtain it—or at least the exertion to make others believe I am somewhat remotely close. Don't worry. I won't go on a tangent about appearing perfect on social media again. Right now, I want to talk about real life.

The entire purpose of this book can be conclusive within this single chapter. It's the antidote against achieving and maintaining false perfectionism—the fuel to embrace the raw, unfiltered, natural version of yourself. In doing so, I am going to break some sour news to you right now, so hang on to your britches. You are not perfect, not even close. Nor am I. If perfect was at the far right, you and I would be about seven left turns in the opposite direction. Did that sound a bit harsh? I do apologize, but hear me out. I want to channel this brassy realization into your mind not to diminish your self-image, but to assist you into the reality that we are so far from attaining perfectionism that we may as well stop trying. Save your energy, girl. It's not our thing. Jesus Christ was, is, and always will be the only One to wear that badge; so stop trying to steal it from Him.

I have always been the type of gal who did not like to be told what to do. That isn't because I chant the independent woman theme song and will have no superiors, nor do I believe that my way or my methods are inferior. Rather, I despised needing to be told how to do something, not having already known how to do it successfully. I always wanted to be the one who had the job done, taken care of, and progressed to the next task without error and without redirection. In my eyes, correction means failure. If I need to be told that I am doing something wrong, then I have utterly fallen. Even as I wrote this book, long before reaching a publishing contract, I agonized anticipating the editing process. I could not accept the criticism. As you can imagine, that failure made me angry with myself. I should have known better, I thought. I needed a perfect score, a solid ten from all three judges. There was no room for nines and sevens.

I'll give you a few examples. While in college during the fall semester of my senior year, I was taking a pharmacology class I had selected as a required elective. It was a rather difficult one with an even more demanding professor, but I worked hard during that course. When midterms quickly approached, we were given an exam on everything we had learned up to that point during the semester. I can still see the questions while flipping through that test—there were fifty of them. A few classes later, when the professor had returned our exams to us, I received mine back with a fat, red letter "A," and I had gotten a 96 percent. Now, mind you, this was not an easy course. I should have stood on top of the desk and did a victory jig, but I didn't. The immediate thought that flashed through my mind was *Why not a 100 percent? What did you miss?* I scanned through the exam frustrated and then mentally punished myself for not getting the two questions right that I swore I knew the answers to. It was madness. I knew I was no Einstein. My SAT scores were nothing to be desired. But I knew that course was challenging, and I demanded perfectionism from myself, if not pretty darn close to it.

Then there was the time when I became a brand influencer for a t-shirt company, which was a huge step outside of my comfort zone. I had gotten the email with the regulations to follow when promoting their brand, and the greatest barrier that made me gulp was "You cannot use filters on your photos; it distorts the color of the clothing." I almost quit right then and there. The first time I shared a photograph with no Lark or Reyes or brightness or contrast adjustments, I about passed out. Then I remembered what I am trying to promote to you. If I am going to convince you that you are fully wonderful just the way you are and that we need to become more raw and real with each other about our appearances and our lives, then who am I to be a hypocrite? How fraudulent would I be if I encouraged you to be comfortable in your own skin, but smooth my own in Photoshop? I wouldn't do that to you; we are in this together. There are enough women posing for perfection; we need more real life. Chances are their grass isn't greener and their skies aren't any brighter; it's just a filter.

I believe the origin of portrayed perfectionism has a double-based root. One, we set our bars way too high for ourselves in order to feel successful; and, two, we want others to have this almost envied perception of us. Now that's not because we think we're all that, but if people want to be more like us, maybe *we* will want to be more like us too. My levels for measuring how successful I am are entirely ridiculous. I set unrealistic goals for myself. It's not because I do not believe I can achieve them by the grace of God, but I make expectations become slavery to my own self in order to be this superstar. Granted, I was slightly more lenient with my private self, for I believed that if only I knew I failed, only I could beat myself up about it. When others knew I failed, oh Jiminy Cricket, I was the letdown of the century. I may as well set out rotten tomatoes for others to launch at me because I am that disgraceful.

They could not know that I ruined dinner, acted like a semi-maniac, sinned with that guy, or have abdominal rolls I can hide my fingers in between when I sit down on a chair. Why? If they knew those parts of me, how would they hunger for anything from me? This was my brain activity that I circumvented for years and years concerning my portrayal to everyone outside looking in. I couldn't let my guard down for anyone to see the imperfect me. Then when I finally got a spark lit under my butt after becoming so incredibly fed up with women around me beating themselves up for no legitimate reason, I said, "That's enough." We as women have been on our cases for not having perfect, manicured lifestyles and juggling fifty-seven acts to make ourselves compatible to Wonder Woman, and enough is enough. How would I make anyone admire me, if they were only seeing the fake me? I wasn't being phony, and I wasn't pretending to be someone I wasn't. I just was only inviting others to see the polished parts of me. People don't relate to that, though, ladies. If we want to learn how to do a smoky eye or tricks to boost our social media platforms, we know where to go for that. I can navigate my way through the World Wide Web to obtain a degree, research a board on Pinterest on how to dress business casual, or read a how-to book on just about any ol' thing. What I want to see, what I want to show you, is that we are all only perfect at one thing; and that is being imperfect.

Huddle up, girls. It's about to get real. Honesty about struggles reaches more hearts than seemingly perfectionism ever will. People relate to empathy, not unrealistic expectations. Moms connect to the mother who didn't brush her kid's teeth this morning because she was too tired more than the one who is chilling with her child in matching clothes at Starbucks. Young women relate to the girl in the beginning of the makeup tutorial with nothing on her face more than the cosmetologist version at the end of the clip. Wives communicate more easily with the gal who drove through McDonald's for her husband more than the one who made her family a five-course meal on a Wednesday evening. That's real life. Those are real women. Those are the moments that need to be shared, not because there is anything wrong with them or because they represent failure, but because they resemble reality for most people. Sometimes you go all out and are a big deal, but a lot of times, you and I are getting by with just getting by. Life is not always a sunset, it often goes unscripted, and our perfect plans frequently end up in confusion and disarray. Girl, need I remind you, it's perfectly okay to not be okay. Have a meltdown. Throw your thirty-some-year-old self on the bed and cry or scream if you need to. Let your kid run around with nothing but a diaper on their head. Dare I say, bask in the ambiance of your family enjoying a ham and cheese sandwich with potato chips smashed inside of it as much as prime rib and potatoes au gratin.

I remember my first night as a married woman having to prepare supper for my husband and myself. I always envisioned me placing these savory dinners for my family each evening, with a simple, though beautiful, tablescape for finishing touches. I had worked late that evening and came home, scurrying to figure out what I could present to my husband for our first dinner in our new home together. I stared into the refrigerator and glared over at the pantry, and all I could establish was that I was exhausted. Cleaning chicken made me want to cry as much as turning the oven on to cook it did. The thought of even getting a mixing bowl out to concoct something made me want to cry even harder. Do you know what that dinner ended up consisting of? Macaroni and cheese with a side of strawberries. Oh, and we didn't even eat it at the table; we sat on the couch. At the time I was mortified. I failed as a woman, as a cook, as a 1950s dream housewife. I was the stench of disappointment. But inevitably, I accomplished the mission of dinner that evening. Food was presented, our stomachs were full, and I even put the cherry on top of the sundae by not washing the few dishes I had used in preparation until the next morning. And do you know what? It felt good. Do you want to know something else? You can't tell anyone this. But the Crock-Pot is my best friend.

I self-talked my mind into accepting that I don't have to always be something out of a *Good Housekeeping* magazine. I don't have to be the girl with the booming career or mass influence. I'm not always going to be the go-to friend or the one you seek advice from. I don't have to wear all of those hats to be impressing to other women. When women look at me, what I want them to know more than anything else about me is that I do not have it all together. I don't always smile. Sometimes I'm grouchy, I don't always dress nice, and I burn homemade croutons almost every single time I make them. I'm a horrific baker, my fears more than often control me, and I have belly rolls that I sometimes squeeze to make my belly button look as though it is talking (guess you didn't need to know that one). I've failed myself and the people I love, and I've failed God more times than He should have forgiven me. But I'm loved, I have value, and I have worth despite all of those factors.

And let me assure you God approves of your weaknesses too. Rather, He takes delight in them. It is in those fragile compartments of your persona where His power shines brightest. That's when He steps in and shows off like the boss that He is. It is when you epically fail that the perfected work of Christ invades and reverses any failure you've done. He counts it null and void. In fact, when you really stop and think about it, we are masters at failing. The best part of that is we were never expected to be anything more than human. You want as less of you as feasible and the most of Him in you as possible.

Now I will never encourage you to just give up, to become a bump on a log with your hands thrown at your side with the constant excuse that imperfection is the reason you do not fulfill your potential. I do not expect that you will stop trying in the name of this book. You're not getting off that easy, girl. What I pray you understand, I beg you from my heart, is to stop trying to present this masked version of yourself to please others when no one is present while you wash your face and look at the real you. They don't see the stress. They don't see the sleepless nights nor everything you've thrown to the side of the room out of the camera's angle for the family portrait. Only you do. You deserve to tear down those perfection walls and stop the show. You owe it to yourself to not have to prove yourself to anyone.

The other morning I woke up and was in desperate need of makeup remover wipes. I admire those of you who can get your makeup off with soap and water. I feel as though I need a firehose at times to get all of my mascara from my eyelashes. It was a cold, January morning and still dark outside, but I needed my wipes to get the little remaining mascara from the previous evening off of my face. I remote started my vehicle, grabbed my jacket, and suited up to leave the house. My sister had asked me if I was stepping into public in my current attire, and I answered, "You bet I am."

Now, my mother, God loves her caring heart, encouraged me months prior, "Baby, you are like movie theater popcorn. You walk into the theater, and you just can't help but get yourself some of that good popcorn." Truthfully, a good mother's love is the closest to God's. So that morning I walked into Giant Eagle at six o'clock in the morning with Grinch fleece pajama pants and a Pocahontas t-shirt with the confidence in my mind, "Aye, I'm movie theater popcorn, baby."

Nonetheless, I proudly walked into the local grocery store with the day before's eye makeup smudged across the bridge of my nose, my Grinch pajamas pants, and my hair tossed in a messy bun with my chunky eyeglasses on. As I checked out, a very sharp woman behind me gazed at my appearance, rather unaccepting. The kind cashier told me she liked my Christmas pajamas, even though it was a month afterward. To really kick off my satisfactory presentation, I unzipped my winter coat showing her my Pocahontas tank top that I was wearing underneath as if I just unveiled a Superman chest. I wasn't embarrassed; I was gratified. I made one woman's nose turn in the air at being dressed so improperly in public, yet I made another one smile because I was candid enough to show her what I really look like in the morning. Yes, I woke up like that. I did not enter the store dressed that way because I don't care about myself, nor did I go into public with pajamas on because I think I'm just that sexy. I did it because it felt freeing. Laugh all you want, girl, but I felt more proud of myself walking in the store knowing people would see me as I rolled out of bed than if I spent an hour and a half applying makeup and curling my hair. I did it because it was a small, menial nudge that was another step in my direction of letting my guard down so that I could more freely be me. So this is where we wrap it up, when I give you some well-rounded advice before moving onto our next endeavor. Are you ready?

I want you to let it go. Let your hair down. Shake it off, Queen Elsa style. Let. It. Go. Life is not perfect, not even close, but you need all of the imperfect, failed plans and altered routes to get you where you need to go. You also need the blemished, unpolished, most-of-the-time-messy version of yourself to become the person you are predestined to be. This world has enough people telling us that we should have this type of body, be that type of woman, have this type of lifestyle, and do those sorts of things. Stop freaking out about freaking out. Freak the heck out if it makes you feel good! The next time you are talking in a group of women, if one of them dares to be candid enough to let you in on her little failure secret, confess with her, "You know what, me too, girl. I am her." I am willing to bet you that you will have deeper, more relatable conversations and connections with other women if you are more vulnerable and honest about your own life. So tell her that your husband is getting on your last nerve, that the shirt she loves you are wearing has a big rip in the back where you tried to tear that annoying tag off, or that your children make you question your sanity. I am raising my glass and toasting to you already, girl. Salute.

It's not about making ourselves look bad, and it's not my goal to create an army of ladies walking around acting like cavewomen. This is about embracing the concept that the things we hide most about ourselves are what we have most in common. You are never going to be perfect, just as I won't. But how stinking amazing it is that we don't have to be.

Things to remember:

- Spoiler alert: Perfection is utterly unattainable. So stop trying while you're ahead.
- You will connect with others more easily by letting them see the imperfect parts of you, rather than the winsome ones.
- You cannot swipe a filter on your life, so don't focus on how it appear to others.
- You are not the only one struggling to figure it out; we all are.
- If Jesus loves you imperfectly, why not try loving yourself that way too? Cut ya' self some slack, wrap your arms around you, and hug tight.

After reading this chapter:

Something that stuck with me is…

_____

_____

_____

_____

_____

Something I want to challenge myself with…

_____

_____

_____

_____

_____

This is how I am going to do it…

_____

_____

_____

_____

_____

My I Am Her statement is…

_____

_____

_____

_____

_____

Chapter 6

The Angry One

In your anger do not sin: Do not let the sun go down while
you are still angry, and do not give the devil a foothold.
—Ephesians 4:26–27

Speak when you are angry and you will make
the best speech you will ever regret.
—Groucho Marx

If there's one thing I've mastered in this life, it's being angry.

I'm quite actually an Olympic gold medalist at being enraged. I've outright perfected the craft of it. To be more truthful, the physical copy of this manuscript took a couple of good 'ol-fashioned beatings in multiple fits of rage. It wasn't personal, just strictly business. When I am mad, I react. It's immediate, it's impulsive, and whatever inanimate object that's closest to me is liable to become a casualty. There's no brewing or stewing period. It's just an accelerated force of nature that goes from frolicking through the meadows to duck and cover; shots have been fired.

Adorable, right? Remember I am honest with you always.

Now I'm sure you are painting a relatively tranquil image of me in your mind thus far, but allow me to further illustrate. Rage and I are the kind of pals that hold hands and galavant in the park together teetering on the swing set. Rather, considering the effect anger has on me, it is more like burning the entire playground down—a Ferris wheel set fire. Hurt, rejection, altered plans, disappointments, people, a slow-moving fast-food drive-through line, and life in general made me angry. I let each negative experience, feeling, or painful memory sink down into the pit of my gut and take fortress there so that when I began to rumble, my entire being shook. Literally, guys, my voice would shake like I was driving over rumble strips and saying, "Ahh."

I was mad at being lied to, angry for being controlled, furious at him for leaving, irritated at her for ignoring me, and irked at the friends who became enemies and the family who became strangers. I was mad at myself. Oh, how much anger I harbored for myself alone. I was irate that I couldn't possess the judgment to see through people better, annoyed I made the wrong choices, and aggravated at how I could be so downright, bona fide stupid so very many times. I discovered a habit of quick-triggered anger within myself that only worsened as I aged. What got me most, though, what ate away at my core like a little Pac-Man in my stomach chomping away to bits, was when people believed or said something about me that was not true. Flip switch. I became the Hulk.

I know what it's like to feel the rage in your fingertips like you've just touched a hot surface and you are about to explode. I understand the emotion of your head feeling physically warm to the touch in such ways that a cool rag is the only thing that could maintain your body temperature. When you want to hit, kick, punch, scream, or flip a car, I get it. I walked around like a volcano bubbling just waiting for the next opportunity to erupt. My outbursts were entirely disproportionate to the circumstance. It was nothing for me to exit my vehicle in the middle of the road to yell at another person whose driving frustrated me. Lashing out on customer service or retail personnel because they made error to my order was a mundane, daily habit of mine. There was a pit in my belly, filled with rage, and it surfaced whenever the opportunity presented itself. My cool would just not keep cool.

Before you go judging, you've been there before too. I'm sure of it. Possibly not quite at my great white shark level, but I am almost certain that you can relate. Things happened. Perhaps someone hurt you, and it ticked you off. Oftentimes things happen between people. Then there's either a minor scuffle or an epic blowup, but none-theless, it sticks. One party believes it happened this way; the other sounds like they attended an alternative scene with different char-acters. You know the saying, "There are three sides to every story, yours, mine, and the truth." You know what I have to say to that?

Blah, blah, blah.

Seriously, though, when you are passionate about your stance and know in your heart what your intentions are, you don't care about that mysterious floating "truth" side. You feel in your heart you *are* the truth, not in the sense that we believe we're oh-so-innocent or our side of the story is always without fault, because none of us are always completely guilt-free. If that were the case, you'd lack human fragility. But when you know your heart, you know what you meant when you said it, you know how you were true in your intentions, and then someone challenges that, game over. I don't know about you, but I did not take that lesson in life so gracefully. I knew I was a good employee, I knew I was a good friend, and I knew I was a good wife. I was not perfect, not even close, but I knew my heart. And when I was challenged by any of those situations, my anger skyrock-eted because people began to depict me in a way that was completely opposite to my being. I felt out of control, like a bystander with my hands tied behind my back and tape over my mouth, defenseless. I knew I had to loosen the reigns and digress my fight because ulti-mately, it wasn't my battle to suit up for. I had to let go, but how?

After my husband had left, I found myself furious with so many, many insignificant situations. That divorce was the ultimate fuel that shot my anger meter to a new level high. For instance, the fact that people did not know the truth of everything that was happening disturbed me. The idea that others might have thought false accusa-tions about myself to be true drove me mad. Knowing that there was absolutely nothing I could do, being completely powerless, made me want to bulldoze dilapidated buildings. I was being eaten alive in my mind by consuming thoughts that so greatly angered me that it was affecting my well-being.

So allow me to explain something to you about this strong emo-tion I am rambling about, being as though I seem to be an expert in it. Anger is like drinking a big, tall glass of poison. And I don't mean the quote about drinking poison and expecting it to harm the other person. Right now, I'm not concerned with the person or entity you are angry with. I'm focused on you. When you drink water, yes, boring water, it nourishes and quenches your body. You need it to survive. So throw a lemon or a cucumber in it to make it more indulging, and drink it. Water is essential, period. Thus, taken in the right quantities, it fuels and propels your body to carry out its necessary functions. Now, if you were to drink a glass full of poisonous substance—please do not test my knowledge—your body would become intensely harmed, probably even lethally affected. Emotionally speaking, this is what happens to our bodies when hosting anger. You are ingesting a nice, big, harmful gulp of dark, thick, tarry poison; and it piles like sediment deep inside.

Now, before we continue and for clarification purposes, if you run into a piece of furniture and become maddened with the object that tainted your pinky toe, I would not classify you to have anger issues. General anger is a human emotion experienced by each and every one of us. Jesus Christ, the perfection of Man, was biblically documented to have been angry. Because He is perfect and we are not, His anger was accounted as being righteous. What I am speaking to is the little anger ball in your belly from 1994 that you are still clinging onto. When you hold onto negative emotions such as this, you extend that offender-paid rent that keeps residency to nag you daily. You might not express your anger on a Tuesday night because you are specifically thinking about those harsh, cold words he said when he left, but they will manifest when you snap on the unfriendly cashier at the grocery store. Just because you are not showing the anger directly related to the hurt doesn't mean that it's not like a little minion fueling and directing your emotions. It may be disguised, but it's dangerous. So let's dig a little deeper past the top soil of the originations of the fury.

As stated prior, my greatest challenge with anger was dealing with the matters of my divorce. If I could be transparent, I am entirely unsure of how many innocent eyewitnesses or blameless objects became the victims of my outrages. It wasn't just because he left or because I had to sell my dream house, although those facts did not help. What made me most angry, more than anything involved in this season, was that I felt like the truth about the situation was snuffed. I'll have you know, though, I was cocked and loaded, ready to inform the masses at all times. When I parked at Walmart, because what other establishment is an epicenter of any given town, my eyes scanned for anyone whom I felt needed to be informed. Can you visualize me? Like a ravenous, frothing at the mouth, rabid dog breathing heavily looking for my prey. I needed a leash.

I wasted a handful of the following months spent in this manner. I became so obsessed with people knowing what *really* happened that every time I grabbed my car keys I was rehearsing one-liners in my mind. Looking back, how incredibly ludicrous was I? I wish I could tell you I had that life-freezing, light bulb moment when it all suddenly made sense to me and I finally gained the right perspective. Truthfully, I could not even tell you when it happened. I just know that it did. I could guess it was somewhere between time progressing and increasing insensitivity to what then seemed to be "old news." Regardless of the time line, God so graciously tended to this beast-like creature I had become, and I finally realized my anger was transforming the person I actually was. This now leads me to lending you a fancy little handout concerning my lessons in dealing with anger, more specifically with wanting to vindicate yourself to maintain your sanity. Consider it a compact memo in which you could briefly skim the bullet points rather than have to figure it out for your own. Trust me this isn't an easy chapter, but it's necessary for us to grow. So dig your heels deep, sis.

First, you do not have to prove yourself nor your side of the story to anyone. The rumor mill will spit out just about anything you can think of, and that's a guarantee. It's like a game of telephone when you whisper in one person's ear, "The big dog ate my hotdog in the park," but the person at the end of the line says, "The frog hates the dark." The evolution of truths passing through person to person almost always gets contorted. What you consider to be absolute truth and undeniable justice, the other party probably believes the same about their stance. Take for instance a Rorschach test. That's the fancy name for the psychological testing composed of inkblots. I take a gander and I may see a dancing hippopotamus, whereas you may see a beached Beluga whale. It's called perspective, people, and we all have different ones. I swore up and down that I was the offended, not the absolute faultless, but I was the wronged victim. Others probably thought differently. And I'm sure they did. In fact, I *know* they did. They had their side and believed they were just as wronged or maybe justified their actions due to their beliefs as much as I had mine. That is an endless debate that is as useless as building a snowman on a beach. So stop wasting your time. There is one Judge, and that is God Almighty, so do not waste your days convincing people who will not be the face staring back at you at the brinks of eternity. It took me many painful nights and wasted days to come to the realization that it doesn't matter my position in the eyes or minds of another. Sure, I care about my reputation, and I aspire to have a high esteem with those I come in contact with or influence. But when I am vesting my entire being into proving myself for others' validation, I've given them a little too much power. If you were wronged, God knows and will vindicate you in His timing. If you did the wrong, God also knows and will forgive you. So carry on, my friend.

Next, if He isn't angry anymore, nor should you be. Phew, this is a tough one. I have never had this conversation with God, but I am more than sure that when His children are hurt or offended, He does not present Himself as indifferent. I have no supernatural telescope into heaven, though I'm willing to bet that when we agonize, when we hurt to our cores and cry ourselves to sleep, He pains with us, as any loving Father would. One afternoon while sitting idle in my car, just myself alone with all of my angry thoughts, I tried to transfer my perspective from my menial, human mind-set to an eternal frame of mind. I reflected upon Jesus and thought of the offenses He was presented with, and I pondered on His responses. Of the most insulting misdeeds Jesus experienced, Judas was among the worst in my opinion. Judas was a disciple, among the twelve elected to be Jesus's followers and anticipated evangelicals to lay the foundation for Christianity. Judas, one of His own, betrayed Jesus, then furthermore led His accusers to find Him fearfully in prayer, and then sealed His identity with a kiss.

I don't know about you, but if that were me, I would have squared up with Judas and said something uber-salty back to him and just about swore him to eternal damnation. This is why I am not Jesus, and He is. Contrary to my presumable justification, Jesus replied, "Do what you came for, friend" (Matthew 26:50 NIV). Erm, what? Did He just refer to him as a *friend?* Let's take it a step further. Not only did Jesus call the man who betrayed Him friend but also He permitted him to fulfill the act of betrayal. He befriended the traitor and in fact encouraged him to accomplish his mission, which led Him to His gruesome death. You may argue, "Yeah, but Jesus knew it was all a part of the master plan. He knew Judas would betray him. In fact He predicted it at the last supper." You're right. But that doesn't mean it still didn't hurt Him, just like what they did hurt you. He was human too. Remember?

I wanted to remain angry. I refused to offer any recompense for the wrong done toward me, but if Christ my Savior can forgive a man before he even felt the remorse of his sin, who am I to cling to the grips of anger toward that person either? Did Christ not forgive me?

I get it. Believe me how I do. You are probably cringing while the painful memories of hurt surface through your mind, and you crumble at the thought of letting go of that anger or resentment. They don't deserve it. I'm sure of it. If I knew your story, I would probably be mad at them too for what they've done to you. The vile, painful things that people do to one another should never be accounted as insignificant or less offensive when we talk about forgiveness. However, in my devotion to you, to you using this anger as a stepping stone for your future, I encourage you to know that God truly does have your back. Jesus is like your Mohammad Ali or Rocky Balboa in the arena of life. He never promised us in this life that we wouldn't take a punch to the face or knee to the ribs. This world and the people in it will beat you down to your knees and leave you black and blue in a pool of pain. I do not doubt that. What you must cling to, though, is that our God never once leaves that ring of life with you. Now I want you to think about what that really means for a moment. Imagine with me the splendor, the justness, of God placing you at His table and preparing for you a setting of glory while your offenders watch. Not for revenge, not for recompense, we're not focusing on the justification or retribution toward the other, though we would more than likely welcome it. He's not a get-back God; He's a setup God. He will use the mud slung on you to form a foundation on which He will place you firmly. It might not be as quick as you'd like, and truthfully, you may not even be aware of how God deals with your offenders. Quite honestly, it's not your business. So this will be something rather difficult to hear.

Sometimes, the truth never gets out. No one will know what you went through, they will not understand what they did to you, your side of the story may never get told to everyone you want it to, and you are going to have to accept that. I know it's not fair; it's not even close to being fair. It's frustrating, it's angering, and you may even hate me a little bit right now. I understand. I'm not speaking that what they did was excusable or you need to be "okay" with the offenses committed toward you. What I am suggesting, rather encouraging, is for you not to let your longing for justice outweigh your shot at freedom. Sometimes not having closure is the only closure you will receive. You must be willing to accept that not every wrongdoing ends in receiving an "I'm sorry." But that is okay, because we need no one's permission to take what they've done to us and transform it into something useful in return and to forgive them long before they apologize. You have to move on for you, for your sake only. If the only reason you want to move forward is to show them how stable you are doing despite what they've done, you're not healed yet. You are better than that; you deserve more than that.

Lastly, and most importantly, I need you to give yourself a break. Take a deep breath in and a slow one out as you speak, "Gabby (your name instead), it's time to let it go." Let go of the anger you have toward yourself—whether it's due to wrongs you've done, sins you've committed, or the people you yourself have hurt. I do not care what it is that has chained you to a boulder of resentment toward yourself; it's time to let it go. And that's an active, daily, step-by-step process we will continue to practice long after you turn the last page of this chapter.

I remember doing an activity with a group of at-risk youth where we physically represented ourselves letting go of our past pains. I participated with the kids and along with them wrote down my innermost feelings on a rock about the size of my fist. Truthfully, I needed a boulder to write down everything I was angry at or afraid of. Once we finished releasing our deepest burdens on this rock, we launched them into a nearby pond signifying we let go of those burdens. Now, I am not knocking any symbolic exercise because I too believe sometimes we need to do something tangibly to push ourselves toward our emotional or mental goals. But truth be told, that exercise was for the Hallmark movies where all the problems are resolved before the commercial break. It's not real life. Does it feel freeing? Of course. But those pains didn't sink to the bottom of the pond with the rock that day. They were still there when I got in the car, still there when I went to bed that night, and still there the next morning. I don't admit that to be discouraging, but to be realistic with you. It's not going to be overnight; it takes time. However, what's just as significant as eventually coming over the top of the mountain of healing is taking the steps upward toward it. It's deciding that you are going to start tracking forward, regardless of all the baggage in your backpack.

So today, I encourage you, perhaps even challenge you, to carry your pack to the foot of the cross and begin to unpack. Unpack the anger, dump out the rage that's resulted from your pains, and relinquish the resent that's settled to the bottom of the bag. What you and what I have been carrying is far too heavy, and it feels too good to not be free. Some things are much, much harder to let go of than others, and you may even hold onto them for a little while longer. That's all right too. Remember this is a marathon, not a sprint. We are an honest sisterhood and will never appear to each other as having everything totally figured out because it's quite literally the opposite. Know, though, that I am kneeling next to you doing some extensive unpacking too. We are in it together, and together, we are going to leave that rugged cross with a lot less than what we came with. When Jesus sacrificed His life there, He didn't do it so that we would never experience pain or never endure sorrow or that we should know a hurt-free life. He laid His life in spite of it in that when you do experience such things, He already canceled out the lasting effects they may have on you. Do not wait for anyone else, much less yourself, to set you free; He already did.

Now, let's start emptying out those bags. I promise you it's gonna feel good.

Things to remember:

- The effects of your anger affect *you* the most.
- Sometimes anger is just hurt wearing a mask.
- Do not give others permission to let their wrongdoing keep you from experiencing freedom.
- A state of anger almost always produces regret. Remember that.
- Only God knows what's been done to you, but thankfully, only God needs to know how to heal you.

After reading this chapter:

Something that stuck with me is...

_____
_____
_____
_____
_____

Something I want to challenge myself with...

_____
_____
_____
_____
_____

This is how I am going to do it...

_____

_____

_____

_____

_____

My I Am Her statement is...

_____

_____

_____

_____

Chapter 7
The Rejected

If the world hates you, keep in mind that it hated me first.
—John 15:18 (NIV)

Every time I thought I was being rejected from something good, I was actually being re-directed to something better.
—Dr. Steve Maraboli

"It's not going to happen. No one knows who you are."

When I stumbled across those words in what would appear to be a "let you down easy" email, I felt like I was in a secret game of dodgeball and just got pelted in the stomach with a swift-moving glob of rubber. I mean in all actuality they were right; no one really did know who I was outside of my small hometown. And even that was a stretch to be honest. But can a girl catch a break with the harsh, blunt reminder? Sheesh.

I've never taken rejection, redirection, and especially criticism well. This might come off rather arrogant, but I didn't like to be told "no" or that I was wrong. As you've learned in previous chapters, it's not because I have this egotistical, extreme confidence in myself (rather, it had always been polar opposite). I just took rejection entirely too personal. It stung deep into my core. Someone telling me an idea that I had thought was level Apollo 13 good was actually *no* good was as though they were pressing a megaphone to my right ear shouting the ways I was stupid. Yet, it happens. We get told to take hike, hopefully in a more diplomatic manner; and rejection happens to us at work, in relationships, and in life in general. We get told we're not loved anymore or let go from a job for poor productivity. We get declined from people or places we are potentially interested in. You get the gist. Someone rejects us because they simply think we are not good enough. Say, for example, the fruition of this book.

The formidable process of book publication was an unknown mystery to me much too ambiguous to comprehend. Not only did I have absolutely no idea where to even begin; I didn't even know who or where to go to find out *how* to begin. After extensive evenings spent with my dear friend, Google, I culminated a list of about five Christian, traditional publishing agencies open to unsolicited manuscripts. I quickly grew exhausted, and to be honest annoyed, at how every publisher demanded different, unique requirements to submit a book proposal. One wanted one-inch margins, or that agency requested an extensive background pertaining to information dated back to my childhood. I mean, seriously, can we just not? Of course I am being a bit theatrical, but I almost threw in the towel early due to my shutter annoyance of just trying to get someone to read my manuscript. I get points for honesty, right? Anyway.

I imagined myself as though I was at a very tranquil pond with hardly any fish and a teeny tiny little fishing pole and plop, in went my bait. The proposals were submitted. I was ready to become quite content in my lawn chair, sip on a diet Coke, bask in the sun, and wait idle while expecting little action.

Until I got a nibble.

I received an email from a reputable publishing company's agent who requested to speak with me directly on the phone at a set of listed times to my convenience. I remember that moment vividly, as I was slouched in the driver seat of a large van waiting on my children to be dismissed from school. No, I do not have seven children. I am however a social worker. I quickly perked up and tore off my sunglasses. Disbelief, shock, and an ample amount of humility immediately invaded my mind. I was astonished that someone actually took a liking to my proposal and shocked that it happened during my first-round drafts. Prior to my submissions, I read countless horror stories of successful authors heaping piles of rejection letters, so that was what I expected to receive as well.

Shortly after I responded to her email, I spoke with the agent on the phone who expressed great interest in my book proposal. She explained that she would be meeting with her team the following week and would be pitching my proposal in hopes of their approval to move forward. My shock value increased exponentially. In less than a week, I received the email I had been eagerly awaiting—the decision. Cue dramatic music.

"The team loved your proposal! They want to go ahead and move forward and think that you could be 'the next (insert book title here).'" To maintain everyone's anonymity, I will refrain from sharing the actual title of said book.

I'm not going to lie to you. I cried.

I had that book they were referring to in my reading collection. I knew exactly where it was located. I had the cover burned into my memory because I frequented it. Now I was eligible to be considered an equivalent to it? No, wait. A colleague to a successful author? Hold on. It gets better.

Not only did they categorize me with an author I greatly respected but also as they published her work as well, they would seek her to write the foreword for my book. You can imagine the waterworks now, right? Flowed like the Nile River.

After I spun around in circles, ugly cried, hugged my mother, and then returned my composure to an age-appropriate level again, I responded to her email with an embarrassing amount of "yes" and "thank you's." Next step was accounting department approval.

The process of appropriating costs for publication took much longer than I expected. To be short, and so as not to bore you, after a long month of waiting, I was blessed with a stamp of approval yet again. As my race toward a publication contract wound down, I was headed toward the finish line. Can you hear *Chariots of Fire* playing in the background? I was flailing about, with a tiresome look on my face while thrusting fist pumps to the air in victory.

Last step was the president of the agency's review and signature. This was it. The project was in the bag. I already was given my end of the contract to sign, and I was nearly touching the pedestal of being a contracted author. It was as though I was floating on top of a hot-air balloon absorbing the excitement and anticipation of the threshold I was about to cross with the wind blowing through my brown hair. And then, a giant, pointy pin came and *pop*. Floating turned to free-falling.

"Gabrielle, there is no easy way to say this," the email began. "The president decided against your project. While he believed the book content was great, he said that no one knows who you are. Build a platform first, and then seek publication."

Uhm, what? Did I just get *Punk'd*? Erm, Ashton, you can come out any time now, please.

To be clear, there was no hidden camera and no celebrity running toward me to laugh hysterically at the succession of pranking me. Remember no one knows who I am. It was just me and my cell phone lit with discouragement.

I sat in my car and read those words over a few times to make sure I was reading them correctly. I cried. But this cry was much different from the former.

Not only did I begin to spiral downward on a slope of heartbreaking disappointment but also in that one single moment, my self-esteem as a writer was entirely shattered. What was I thinking? They're right. No one knows who I am. I'll never become a successful author. I'm nobody. It's not going to happen. Never. Give it up, Gab.

While I knew that was just one company, one failed signature, one disappointing email, and one human who didn't believe in me, my hopes fell just a little too short that time.

The most regretful mistake that I had made that day was not wallowing in self-pity, though that was a contending runner-up. That day I shut the door on my dream, closed my laptop, and would not revisit my writing aspirations until almost three years later. I listened to my pitiful self; I gave in, and I gave up.

I've warned you rejection is a particular enemy for me. I take it disproportionally personal. The president of the publishing company thought I was a no one; my esteem crushed. That one guy I went out on a date with who later told me "I'm not sure how to communicate with girls whom I don't really have any interest in" made me feel utterly undesirable. Yes, some guy actually said that to me if you're wondering. I was the girl who was always second best and the last one chosen. I simply was just not good enough. I took rejection from people so personally that I kept their opinions of me like a little pin stuck to my attire to wear around always looming about. Only these pins were not at all displaying an achievement or badge of honor that I had received for helping a little old lady across the street. They were critiques, embarrassment, hurt, and rejection attached to my self-image. You know that elementary grade saying that goes something like "I am rubber and you are glue. Whatever you say to me bounces off and sticks to you"? Ha. Yeah right, not for this girl. I wasn't just the white, drippy glue that's fun to play with on your fingers. I was rubber cement, baby. Every single negative word spoken to me stuck, and it stuck hard. Like the outdoor sticky tape used to trap insects, I was coated with others' opinions of me. And truthfully, I navigated most of my decisions and actions based off of whether I believed others would accept me or not. Take blogging for example.

I cannot tell you (seriously I lost track) how many times I created a new blog or webpage, registered another domain, or enrolled in monthly package plans to share my writing. I probably have my own little portal floating around the World Wide Web in a digital world of similar domain names that have now been deactivated. In retrospect, it can be concluded this be the reason it was so daunting of a task to build a platform for myself. I didn't want the attention; I wanted to remain anonymous. It was safe that way. If they hate me, they don't know who is behind the computer. If they love me, God gets the glory anyway. It was a win-win type of situation.

I remember composing a new Facebook page that I had full intentions of remaining anonymous. In no way, shape, or form did I want my name attached to it at all, bar none. I would manage the content, but no one would know whom it belonged to. Clever, right?

I spent an entire evening creating the page, specifying the content in the About Me section, uploading the profile picture, blah, blah. You know the drill. I even researched countless logo websites to create a little insignia for my secretive account. What I hadn't known, though, was that when I requested for people to like the page, it would appear as so:

"Gabrielle Elisco has invited you to like their page, _____."

Sink ship. *No way, not happening, not today, not tomorrow, no platform for me,* I thought. I even bartered with God that if He willed for the success of my writing, He would just have to get it out there Himself. I was horrified of people receiving that notification, snickering at the thought of what I was inviting them to be a part of, and then completely dissecting my words to meaningless nothings. Embarrassing enough, I had an entire theatrical movie playing in my head. This girl would screenshot my content and send it to that other girl, and they would howl at my attempts. People would ask each other what I was even thinking trying to give advice to others or make myself vulnerable for the world to see. They would say something like "Did you hear? Gabby wrote a book?" Insert eye-rolling. I was not going to let that happen. Too risky. I was afraid to even try. Sure, there was the chance that it could be the complete opposite of my fears and it would be a successful endeavor, but I was way too much afraid to risk failure and the sting of rejection yet again.

This pathetic mind-set I am sharing with you, well, it was my dwelling place for years. I sat on the sidelines, safe and sound, no risk of being hurt and humiliated by people. Yet, I wanted to be effective in God's kingdom. I reminded Him over and over and over again to use me as His vessel and let His spirit flow through myself to others so they could experience the love that He showed me. I wanted to share Him with people, but I didn't want to be shared with people. So we've found ourselves a little conundrum, haven't we?

How could I play it safe and remain secretively hidden, but reach the hearts of God's people? I couldn't do both. So I had to weigh out my options. On one hand, I would remain silent, safely in my comfort zone, and just maybe pray for people from afar or make anonymous social media accounts to encourage them. However, that sounds somewhat creepy. On the other hand, I could get my sorry butt off of the bench, step into the game, and show the crowd what I got. Some may think I'm worthless; others may think I'm worthy enough to lend their attention, perhaps if even just for a moment.

So which to choose?

Let me first inform you from experience being used by God often challenges you to take a leap out of your cozy corner. So spoiler alert! Nevertheless, I began the trek.

The deeper I engaged in my obedience to the Lord to follow what I believed He desired, the more I had to focus on no one else but Him. That took a great deal of self-talk. "So what if they think you are crazy? Who cares if not everyone agrees with you? God knows your heart. Do you care much about anyone else?" Those thoughts may sound a bit crude to the rest of the human population, but they became necessary for me to focus on my goal. My goal was focused on being able to help people, rather than being afraid of what they thought of me. If I remained afraid, I would become less effective to those whom I was destined to reach all because I feared offending those whose rejection technically did not matter.

Now, because I must always clarify myself, I am no one to encourage an I-don't-give-a-hoot attitude about what they think of me and not representing Christ. Remember God's greatest commandment boils down to one thing: love. Rather, we must not become so consumed of people's thoughts about us that it overpopulates what God *knows* about us. We'll talk about that more later.

Writing this book was not difficult in the sense of composing words, although it had its moments, but the outcome I was anticipating was what held me back. In my mind, it was mandatory that it succeeded. I must sell substantial copies. I need good reviews. I have to make my way to the New York Times Best Seller list (go ahead; I allow you to laugh at that one). I was like a robot booping, beeping, and bopping for success.

The demand for the book flourishing wasn't for fame; it surely was not for money because that was the least concern I had when I sought to become an author. It was that I quantified my effectiveness with the measure of its impact I had on others. I had the wrong vision. I wanted success for self-validation, not for kingdom promotion.

Then finally came the day when I needed a mental pause. I slouched down in my chair before my computer, and as I start all refreshing moments, I took a giant, deep, from-the-belly breath. Go ahead. Do one with me now. It's refreshing.

Now exhale. Here's what it boiled down to.

Every single person in this planet, the individual, matters to God. Not groups, not just book clubs, and not crowds of people, the individual has unspeakable importance to the heart of God. We cannot fathom that in our human capacity. If no one else in the world is concerned about rejection other than you, then it still matters to Him. That, my friend, is why He will eagerly leave the ninety-nine sheep to save the one (check out Matthew chapter 18 if that threw you off a bit). The "one" will always be colossally important to Him. Keep that in mind.

So in the words of Tay-Tay, I shook it off. I let all the preconceived obsessions of failure, rejection, pity, and fear fall from me like dropping flies. And I wrote for you.

Yes, you.

If only you, one single person, benefits or reaps welfare from anything in this book alone, just one sentence even, then I will consider it a success. If I sell just one copy and the love of God reaches into your heart, I have achieved my goal. It's not about me; it's about you. If my heavenly Father God is so desperately encapsulated with the concern of your well-being, then as your sister, I am too. And to me, and surely to Him, you are *well* worth it.

There was a stranger who sought me years ago via social media who had been given a prophetic vision to share with me. She wasn't a psychic or a fortune-teller. If she was, I would have immediately blocked her and pleaded the blood of Jesus on my MacBook Air. Trust me. This chick doesn't roll like that. But there are Christians who are blessed with the gift of prophecy, and it is a special token from the Lord. How you know whether they are legitimate or not is that their word will always align with the Word of God and His character and they are completely Holy Spirit led.

She was a kind-hearted woman, a sister in Christ, whom the Lord used to fellowship with me. This woman was searching the internet for Christian ministries for her daughter and stumbled upon the one I was a contributing writer for. She had approached me as a complete stranger, admitting that her greeting might be considered a bit unexpected. And it was. I was taken aback to have had shared such an elaborate illustration from a stranger across the country. She began to share this depiction with me of a woman in a river, joyfully playing along the riverbank and submerging into the waters. Her joy was contagious, and many women ran down to the shores of the river and joined her. There were others, though, who stepped toward the bank of the water, but turned away withdrawing from those in front of them and leaving discouraged. As I concluded reading through this imagery, she encouraged me to plunge into the river waters and experience joy, not minding whether I sought others' approval or not. For months and even years to follow, I had revisited her message and wondered what this message from a complete stranger had represented. There were so many ideologies that I attached as a possible explanation for what this could have meant. Yet what I realized through years of feelings of inadequacy, condemnation, and fear was I began to become that woman who just let my toes dip into the waters, but never dove in. I wasn't playfully splashing in the river, letting my joy flow along the rippling waters. I was the woman on the banks, watching in adoration of the others embracing their freedom and finding fulfillment in their lives. I eventually was on my way to rising and walking away from the shoreline entirely.

Then, I mustered what little bit of courage I could find within myself, and I got my toes wet and then my ankles and then my calves and then my knees; and the more and more I stepped into the waters, unafraid of all the voices telling me a hundred reasons I shouldn't just plunge deep, I discovered the joy in the splashing. Sometimes it gets messy; other times people get upset because you're stirring their waters too much and they like the complacent stillness. But I decided that I much rather invite and encourage others to jump in and enjoy the refreshing waters with me, rather than show them that it's okay to rest along the shoreline. I don't want that for you, and you don't either. I want to be the girl who makes you want to dive in and splash around.

So if you're afraid that they will reject your ideas, pitch it to them anyway. If you fear you will become tongue-tied speaking to them, God will give you the words to say. If you tremble because they might not think your voice is good, sing your heart out anyway. Whatever your passion, be it a fashion blog, cookbook, or album—the sky is the limit—go for it. You matter to someone, and your gift that God has placed within you was made to produce flames that ignite the heart of someone else.

I know it's scary clicking the Publish Now button on your website or social media page. We become vulnerable to entrust the world with something so precious and delicate to ourselves, fearing their acceptance or disproval of what we hold dear. Don't let it hold you back. If one person gains from your passion, throw your chin up in the sky and push those shoulders back. Tip your hat off to yourself because guess what? You just made a difference in the life of someone. Oh, and don't you dare belittle what you are doing. Honey, I'm not talking about mass productions like inventing the cure to smallpox. I'm talking to the girl who makes t-shirts or paints cabinets. I'm talking to the girl who encourages others to exercise and be fit. Oh and you, sis, who is afraid to film a video of herself applying makeup to sell products that make you feel beautiful, I am talking to you too. There's another woman who is going to buy your t-shirt and get a compliment over it that makes her feel good about herself. There's a woman who doesn't have the energy or might be too depressed to exercise whom you're encouraging to get off the couch. There's a young girl who has no idea how to contour her face because in fact it took me about twenty-six years myself to figure that out, but you've helped her feel beautiful.

Do not let the fear of people who do not follow your niche taint it for the ones who are already in your circle counting on you. It doesn't matter if your circle is small. Remember Jesus started out with only twelve.

Now before we end this chapter, I feel the necessity to let rejection have its single moment of redemption. Let's switch gears for a quick moment; you know, cut it some slack. Rejection is not always a bad thing, though that was even painful for me to say. I won't lie. I just spend thousands of words convincing you how much I despise rejection, and now I'm beginning to shed some light on its importance. I promise I'm not a hypocrite, and we have not come thus far in vain. Just hear me out.

While I continue to figuratively sling mud on the word "rejection," I want to highlight when rejection is actually God's redirection. Yes, even rejection can have its moments. When I was graduating from college, I specifically placed in my mind the agency where I wanted to work. I researched the organization and had paid strict attention to their "Now Hiring" section of their website for the duration of my senior year in college. I had applied to that agency probably three different times for various positions, both prior to and even after graduation because I could not let this preconceived notion out of my mind. I presumed it would be my dream job. I never got a callback there, though I couldn't understand why. I exceeded every requirement, I even knew people who worked there, and I always found myself asking God, "Why not?"

When I was sitting in rehearsal for my college commencement, days before receiving my sociology degree, I received an email from the department secretary notifying graduating seniors of a vacant position at a local agency I knew nothing about. I rushed my resume there within the next hour because I could not imagine not having the next step after graduation strategically planned within my mind. I would end up being hired within the next month and quickly began my career as a foster care social worker. That very agency has become my place of employment for a few years shy of a decade now—a place I call home and where I've met lifelong friends, a place that I could not have imagined a more fitting environment for me to work. Rejection was for better redirection. I placed an offer on a house that did not get accepted, only to find a better, more beautiful one. Rejection was for a better redirection. And a failed marriage has led me to a love I've never before known. Rejection was for a better redirection.

Sometimes, rather oftentimes, what we perceive as being shot down, rejected, and thrown into the hypothetical trash can is often redirecting us in the direction of exactly where we're supposed to be going. Those unanswered prayers or "no" prayers are disguised as

God protecting us from the things we believe we want and giving us much, much better.

So, girl, when it comes to rejection, we have three options: 1) be entirely fearful of it and avoid it at all costs, 2) face it head on and let not the fear of those rejecting you stop your dreams, and 3) recognize it as redirection from God. Learn from me, sis, and do not waste your days, even years, raising your hand for option number 1. Recognize rejection for what it really is: fuel or protection. Let it motivate you enough to stand tall or humble you enough to fall on your knees in thankfulness.

Soar. Splash. Jump. Take the leap. You may receive a no, and you may receive it multiple times, but that's all right. Let people scoff. Let others judge. It's merely just opinions and nothing more. Brush yourself off, and get back on your feet again. The world needs *you*. Besides, you never know what the outcome of your best efforts mixed with the power of God within you may produce. With Him, you are utterly limitless. And when the answer is still no, just hang tight, and know that God is straying you from destruction to reconstruction.

What if on the other side of your fear is everything you've ever dreamt you would become? Go ahead. I dare you.

Things to remember:

- Not taking a risk will be your greatest risk and your worst regret.
- Do not let the fear of rejection refrain you from your God-given direction.
- Sometimes rejection is a way of God protecting what He has not willed for you.
- Get up and try again, regardless of what they think.
- Never let the fear of striking out keep you from playing the game. (Babe Ruth said that one, not me.)

After reading this chapter:

Something that stuck with me is...

_____

_____

_____

_____

_____

Something I want to challenge myself with...

_____

_____

_____

_____

_____

This is how I am going to do it...

_____

_____

_____

_____

_____

My I Am Her statement is...

_____

_____

_____

_____

_____

CHAPTER 8

The Man-Obsessed One

*Do not love the world or anything in the world. If anyone loves
the world, love for the Father is not in them. For everything
in the world—the lust of the flesh, the lust of the eyes, and the
pride of life—comes not from the Father but from the world.*
—1 John 2:15–17 (NIV)

*I was too much and not enough for a man who
was everything and nothing at all.*
—Jessica Katoff

'Tis time we part ways, stupid, little, pink hearts emoji.

C'mon, girl. I know you know what I'm talking about, something that only we millennials would share this common knowledge in. You know, when you take the cute little heart or another assigned character once attached to his name.

Ouch, that burns, doesn't it?

Can we just take a moment to make fun of ourselves for a bit? For real, though, you have to laugh at yourself sometimes. I think it's rather healthy to do so. How petty of a generation have we become that we hold our phones in our hands weeping and blubbering snot balls as we click backspace over our little pink or red hearts tagged to our once beloved's name. Ugh. I disgust myself when I visualize the many times I've done that.

I am almost embarrassed to share this chapter with you, but I feel that I must. I'm not happy to admit to the world that I spent decades being boy crazed or obsessed with having a relationship in my life at all times. Truthfully, after one relationship had ended, while in the midst of my weeping over changing name statuses in my phone, there was a lingering thought in the back of my mind considering, *Who's going to be next?* Golly, I sound so desperate. It is imperative, though, for me to be completely transparent should it be helpful to you, even when it makes me appear a little coo-coo-ca-choo.

I started dating when I was at the age of thirteen. Quite frankly, I'm unsure we can define that as legitimate courtship being that the majority of communication was via AOL instant messaging. Nonetheless, that was when I had my first boyfriend. This was the time when you waited for the bell to ring so that you had those four minutes in the hallway of making sure your hair looked perfectly fluffed for when he passed you in the hallway. I'll be fair now and cut myself a bit of slack here deeming my age and teenage hormones to the boy-crazed obsession. So let us fast forward a bit, say, to my early twenties. That seems like a realistically mature and appropriate place to begin.

So there's this guy (as most of these stories begin), and he's totally dreamy. And he was. His charm was completely galvanizing, he had a smile that accentuated his perfectly sculpted jawline, and I was totally into him. Aside from his obvious physical attributes, I was most interested in what I thought he represented as a man, strength, godliness, faithfulness, a slight arrogance even, though I was utterly infatuated. I remember the first day I had laid eyes upon him, and I just had to know more. So I approached him, and after introducing myself, I made it evident that I was rather interested in him and suggested we should meet for coffee sometime. Ha! Just kidding. I dove, hid, and commenced the Facebook stalking, because that's much, much more appropriate, right?

I never was the type of gal to make the first move. I would not attribute that to being cocky, but the fear of being turned down. Avoiding that horrifying fear becoming a reality, I waited for him to come to me. Real quick, let's think of a name to call him for the sake of his anonymity and to spare myself from having to come up with creative ways to refer to him. How about "Bo"? Not that exciting, but we'll keep it simple.

So Bo and I met one fine day via his suggestion of course, and I was hooked immediately. He played the hard to get game and seemed totally uninterested in me, but that somehow never dulled my interest in him. Being that I am a rather impatient person, I did not plant all of my eggs in one basket, so I dated in the meantime. All the while, though, I never forgot about Bo. After a few years had passed, we began chatting again and eventually spent some time together. Could this finally be happening? Hanging out turned into holding hands, awkward side hugs turned into our first kiss, and we eventually began dating. Insert happy, ugly cry here. I had thought I just received the prized hog that every other girl must have been coveting. Listen. Homeboy had it going on (or so I thought). He was everything I had presumed that I wanted in a man, and being that I had my eye on him for so long, it was like I finally reached my man goal after so many idle years. That one fall evening, when he asked me to be his girlfriend in a completely unromantic way might I add, though I couldn't have cared less, I finally got to call him my very own. Ah, alas.

I presumed our relationship would be something like Judd Nelson thrusting his fist through the air in victory because he got the girl. In fact as I write this, my foot is tapping to the beat of "Don't You" by the Simple Minds. To my surprise, though, I was not on the set of a remake of *The Breakfast Club*. Shocker.

Somehow, somewhere along the road to recreating a romantic chick flick, my plot started to resemble a horror film. Rewind. That was a bit over the top. There was no bloodcurdling screaming or chasing monsters with axes. Nor was I dating a serial killer. However, that relationship was the furthest thing from a romantic comedy with a five-minute issue being resolved by a kiss. In fact, it was totally opposite of what I formerly dreamt it would be. It was further away from my ideations than the sun is from Pluto. Am I painting a clear picture here? Oh, and it didn't take long until I and everyone around me realized I was completely miserable—frightfully miserable. When I think back to that relationship, I shudder a bit and give my head a quick shake, as if I could shed the memories. Yet the worst part of the entire experience was that I had no idea what happened to myself. Who on God's big ole earth was this new version of me that overtook my mind and heart? I became one of "those girls."

I have always been a pretty outspoken, speak-my-mind, Italian type of woman. Did you see how I tried to put some of the blame on my heritage there? If you said or did something that upset me, you knew about it in less than .032 seconds whether that be through glares or tears. I'm not at all vicious and I hate confrontation; rather, I abhor it. I just tell it like it is. For some reason, though, I let Bo get away with absolutely whatever he wanted to. I was second best, never considered, disrespected, neglected, and hidden in the shadows like I was the hunchback of Notre-Dame. It was the type of relationship you'd encourage your girlfriend to escape from during a girls' night over some pizza and Riesling. But I stayed. And because I stayed, because I set the standards of that treatment as being acceptable, Bo continued his shenanigans; and it got worse.

Our relationship came to the point of hardly speaking, and I felt as though NASA's technological blueprints would have been easier to discern. As I reflect on that time during my life, I wish I could have duplicated myself and have my clone kick my own rear end and knock some God-given sense into me. Realistically speaking, being that we do not have time machines or cloning devices, that's virtually impossible.

So you may be asking yourself why I stayed in that awful relationship. What was she gaining? Why did she allow herself to be treated that way? So he seemed to be all that and a bag of crinkle-cut potato chips, big deal? You know, I ask myself the very same thing. I have absolutely no idea why I tolerated such mistreatment, and I still could not give you a legitimate answer. However, one day, one altering afternoon in a disgusting public bathroom, I caught an epiphany.

In the predominantly Italian-American hometown I reside in, there are some words that our people have cultivated on their own. You won't find them in a dictionary, I promise you, but I'm here to give you some exclusive vocabulary to add to your dialogue. Imagine an utterly disgusting entity by which you are repulsed and so beyond "grossed out" that you feel the immediate need to get into a shower and scrub the epidermis off of your body. There's a word for that. We call it *scheive*.

And this bathroom I was in, oh, did I scheive it.

Regardless of the stink around me and the filthy black floors that must have been white at one time or another, I got down on my knees, desperately, and I cried out to God from a disgusted place— figuratively and literally, that is. In that moment I found myself in, I was distraught, broken down, and exasperated from feeling as worthless as those funky bathroom tiles. But I still didn't want to let Bo go. What was wrong with me? I had imagined what it would have been like to be with him for so many years, and it was finally a reality for me, though a nightmare; yet I *still* wasn't ready to give God permission to take him out of my life. It's not that He needed it, but God is a gentleman after all. I remember my heartfelt prayer, "Lord, if you present me with the opportunity, I will stand up for myself. I will stand up to him whether he leaves or stays." That was tough for me. I know that sounds nauseatingly despicable and pathetic, but it's the truth. Deep down I knew what I was speaking into existence. I knew a relationship wasn't supposed to be this way, especially a godly relationship. As I rose from that dirty floor, I looked into the mirror, and I saw myself in a completely different way. I do realize that may sound like a rom-com sappy moment; but, girl, I kid you not. It happened. It was like a little gray storm cloud over my head went poof and a little sun began to dance in its place. I looked at myself, as if my body and the reflection in the mirror were two different people, and I said, "You don't deserve this."

And I actually believed it.

We've all heard that pep talk a time or two, or ten, in our lives and probably extended that line of empowerment to another. It's entirely overused. But for the first time in my life, I finally accepted it. For the first time since my eyes fell upon that boy, I now recognized that it didn't matter how badly I wanted that formerly perceived relationship. What mattered was that I did not deserve the reality it had succumbed to. And when, oh when by the way, did I subject my worth and integrity to the presence of a man?

Within the next hour after that courageous, for me at least, prayer, God had granted me the opportunity I had requested from Him, and our relationship ended—just as I thought it would. Within one text message recanted, where I actually presented myself as a real human being with real emotions, I received a paragraph back confirming what I already knew would be the response. But I didn't just lose a man in that moment. I felt I regained myself again. And it felt good to have her back. I missed her.

It felt good to finally express my feelings and my opinion to someone who got a hall pass to stomp all over them. I felt proud that I finally could not care less whether he was in or out of my life, but that I loved me more. Most importantly, it didn't matter if it did not matter to him; it mattered to me, and that's all that mattered. Did you catch that? Simply put, I mattered more than what he thought I did. You could imagine I gave myself a mental smack in the face and said, "Good to have ya back, kid!"

I later developed this theory in my mind we as women tend to do in efforts to win the affection and/or attention of a man. I like to call this philosophical phenomenon "conforming and staging." I hope you didn't get too excited; it's not exactly Aristotle level. However, I saw a trend forming in myself that I patented in hopes I'd win their hearts. I conformed to who I thought they wanted me to be; and I staged myself, my life, into what I presumed looked appealing to them as well. If I knew they were into fitness, I oh so suddenly grew a passion for the art of physical activity and became a gym guru. Girl, my definition of working out is lifting the top cover of the pizza box open. That's my bicep exercise. Who was I kidding? I wasn't a marathon runner. Heck, I get out of breath running up a few flights of steps. I believed, though, that the more appealing I made myself to that specific man, the more I liked what he liked, the more he'd want me. The only problem was it wasn't *me*. And the more I began to alter the person I truly was, the more unrecognizable I became.

So here's a bit more about me. This may sound like a profile biography for Match.com, but you get the heart of the matter. I hate seafood. I don't like to sweat. My extent of being outdoorsy is walking to my car, and sometimes even that makes me irritated when

I frantically swat a bug out of my personal space. I desire to know absolutely nothing about *Breaking Bad* and never watched a single episode in my life. Sometimes I like to buy something expensive for myself because I work hard for my money, and most times I buy clothes from consignment stores because they're cute and affordable. I am not going to apologize nor change who I am for you, for him, for no one. Sorry 'bout your luck, Chuck. This is me. I am her.

And I want you to know something too. Just as I am me, you are you. And you don't have to change yourself for any man, honey. You are the cherry on top of the sundae, the "mic drop" in any affirmative statement, and crème de la crème. I do not care if he has money in the bank, a balla crib, or a six pack you can wash clothes off of. If you have to change who you are to make him love you, he just ain't the one, sis.

You are good enough. You are pretty enough. You are smart enough. You are successful enough. You, yes, you, are one heck of a catch. And if Tim didn't see it, if John didn't notice it, if Bo didn't recognize it, and if Joe took advantage of it, it's simply their loss and truly your gain—because not every man is going to treat you like you are the best thing since sliced bread. And quite actually, that's okay. It does not matter if fifty men didn't treat you right; the difference is when just one does. But even still, you are sufficient to stand alone until he should come along. In the meantime, we mustn't fall into the trap of yearning the love of a man who considers us as important as his protein powder. Know this: The right one will recognize your worth without you having to try to display it. You will not have to put on a musical showcase to convince him to invest his time in you. There are those jerks who will hurt you, and it's inevitable. There is no denying that. But if they were not the Man Who created you, then they can't break you, either. Do not do what I did for the majority of my youth—allow my mistakes to be not taken in vain. Oh, the amount of time I wasted on obsessing over all the wrong men to love me. If I wasn't wasting my time crying over them, I was devising a plan to make sure they knew what they were missing out on. I allowed the addiction of either making them want me or sorry they lost me that I ran this fixation like a side job.

GABRIELLE ELISCO

I have dated a considerable handful of men, and I have found that I am able to compartmentalize them into two different categories. I was either not good enough for them or too much for them. Either I didn't live up to their standards and I was their ninth draft selection or they were too intimidated by the woman I am. Okay, Gabby, so what's the solution then, you say? How do we become the happy medium that men desire? Well, for starters, ditch the idea that you need to become anything a man wants you to be, rather than who God already created you to be. Sure, we are always striving to change for the better and evolve into more refined versions of ourselves, and I encourage you to do so. But if you are taming your awesomeness so he feels more of a man or overwhelming yourself so that he deems you're enough of a woman, excuse yourself like the lady boss you are and walk away. You are better than that.

So, all this being said, I want to resonate deep within you, to the center of your identity. Mind you, this chapter is not a dating self-help book that will guide you through the do's and don'ts of dating. Right now, we are focusing on you—single, individual, you. Now pay close attention. You will never, I promise you never, find your fulfillment in a man or his opinion concerning yourself. Oh sure, he can give you the butterflies and the goosebumps, but so can a rollercoaster ride or a sale at Nordstrom. Whether you are single, dating, engaged, married, divorced, or whatever your relationship status may be, I am here to exclaim from the theoretical rooftops to you that your value is so much more than subjecting yourself to being treated anything less than royalty. You are a princess, because your Father is a King.

May you never find yourself so consumed by a man that you begin to alter the divine woman God crafted you to earn men's validity. I can promise you right now that there will be men of your past and possibly men in your future who will not treat you good enough or think you are worth their time. True maturity and wisdom, and acceptance of loving who you are, is not caring whether or not they think you're worth it. It's simply knowing beyond a shadow of a doubt that you already are.

My mother used to remind me of this illustration from the time I began dating until present day. "Baby," she would begin, "you are the cake; he's just some frosting. The cake is still delicious with or without the frosting." And she's right. I mean, sure, the frosting adds a decadent sweetness that complements the cake well; but truthfully, the cake can stand on its own and still be deliciously ravishing.

That's you, my friend. Whether you are funfetti or red velvet cake, you are scrumptiously appetizing with or without him. Now I'm not suggesting we go on an independent women rampage pledging our disgrace with the male species. This surely is not my vow to remain single just to not give into the conformities *some* men have placed on women. Notice I said some, not all. I am very selective of my usage of language, and I must encourage you to be aware that we do not speak of all men. Fortunately, there are still some noble ones out there, and you will notice them when you see the fruit they are producing—how they speak to you, how they regard your emotions, and how they praise you for the woman that you already are rather than encouraging you to become someone you are not. The right man won't let you lose who you are, but simply being with him will remind you more and more of yourself. And he will love you and cherish every bit of that woman.

In that aspect alone, he will resemble the love of Christ.

After experiencing abandonment, I would constantly cry out to God in fear, petrified of the thought of dating again. I had just been hurt so deeply, so preposterously, that the thought of suffering from another heartbreak felt as though it would be the straw that broke the camel's back. "Lord," I would mutter through tears, "how am I going to know whether a man is the one for me or not?" I thought I was so very sure on my wedding day that I held hands with the one I was destined to be with. I did not want to go back to that person I was and fall into the traps of being so discouraged that I began to confirm to the desires of the different men I would meet. I let thoughts swarm through my mind like bats escaping out of a cave, when the stillness of the Holy Spirit quieted my heart and reminded me, "He will most resemble Me."

Ah-ha. That's the ticket. The man who is destined to be mine will resemble the Man Who loves me the most. I won't have to be perfect, because Jesus loves me despite the mess that I am. I won't have to chase his love, because Jesus seeks my heart daily. I absolutely will not have to obsess over becoming who I think he wants me to be, because Jesus loves me already for everything I've been, everything I am, and all that He knows I have yet to become.

That's him, sis—the man who emanates the love of Christ. He is "the one."

But even if you have not met him yet, although you may be awaiting his arrival, stop obsessing over anyone else but Jesus. If you want to become infatuated with a man and eat, sleep, and breathe his existence, choose Jesus. Obsession over Him is the only fixation that will never lead you with emptiness and a broken heart. Let His love rest on you like the morning dew, and let His gaze upon you be the only eyes you are concerned with staring back.

You will never find fulfillment or satisfaction in mere men. But I promise you you will discover everything you ever dreamed, and more, in Him.

Things to remember:

- Never, ever, compromise yourself to meet another's standards.
- Remain loyal to who you are and refuse to alter anything about yourself just to make a man happy.
- A man is meant to be your helper, not your maker. So stop giving him the same accreditation as Jesus.
- The end of a man is not the end of your world.
- Men may come and go, but Jesus never will.

After reading this chapter:

Something that stuck with me is...

_____

_____

_____

_____

_____

Something I want to challenge myself with…

_____
_____
_____
_____
_____

This is how I am going to do it…

_____
_____
_____
_____
_____

My I Am Her statement is…

_____
_____
_____
_____
_____

CHAPTER 9

The People Pleaser

Am I now trying to win the approval of human beings, or of God? Or am I trying to please people? If I were still trying to please people, I would not be a servant of Christ.
—Galatians 1:10 (NIV)

I can't tell you the key to success, but the key to failure is trying to please everyone.
—Ed Sheeran

I am terrified of you not liking me.

Well, at least the old me was. I am a now recovering people pleaser, but admittedly I sometimes revert back to my previous ways of needing your acceptance.

For real, though, if we are going to continue on this bandwagon of being completely honest with each other, I would be diving off, tucking, and rolling down a steep hill if I said I wasn't afraid of you thinking I am just a wannabe, small-town loser who's somehow offended you. Don't say I didn't warn you. I am a work in progress.

Ever since I was a child, I was vastly concerned with what people thought of me. I'm not sure where that obsession began being that it dates back to further than my memory serves, but it's been such a stinkin' pest. Sure, I had progressed and healed from the obsession of accepting myself solely based on what I thought of me, but this was different. This was about what I thought of myself concerning how others viewed me. I could be in a room filled with 999 people who were waving banners for me, but one straggler in the corner who disliked me, and that huge crowd would become invisible. They hardly mattered. I would hone in on that one single hater and figure out what I had to do to win them over. Cookies? Pie? Amazon gift card? What do I have to do? Think I'm goofy all you want, but it would crush my heart into a hundred little fleshy pieces when I knew someone disproved me. I constantly feared upsetting someone else that I always took a second runner-up position to my own emotions. I downright lay on my back like a dog in submission, all in efforts to ensure that you were pleased, regardless of how I felt.

I can physically be seated here writing these words right now and close my eyes imagining the ways in which I used to operate. There was little Gabby, oh, little vibrant girl with her hair constantly slicked back in a tight ponytail, who chased another little girl around the playground because she was mad at her for not choosing her in tag. That seriously happened. I really did chase after another girl in circles because I apparently hurt her feelings. It stuck in my brain to this day, and I can still visualize her little face crunched with anger trying to dodge me as I sought reconciliation. Might I add, home-girl was fast. I continued chasing others, now more figuratively than literally; and once I got to high school, then college, and even the workforce, it grew more intense. If I knew a friend in eleventh grade was in a bad mood that day, I went out of my way to ensure I was in her good standing. If a co-worker was cranky, I had to be certain it was not pertaining to something I had done or not done. That boyfriend who didn't call me back for days at a time, I let him get away with thinking that I approved of that behavior. I can clearly see teenage me tapping the screen of the phone to see if they replied yet. "Were they mad? Or were they just busy? Crap, I shouldn't have made that comment. Maybe I alluded to something, and they are upset now. Or maybe I should have said something supporting them in front of the other girls so they knew I was on their side. You know what, let me just text them again, maybe send a funny meme, and break the ice; and then I can feel them out. Of course in the mean-time, I will be anxious and cranky with an upset stomach because I'm a nervous wreck about it." That right there was my daily ritual.

And this is when you have my permission to cup your hand over your mouth and roar "Patheeetic," but if someone offended me, I *still* was the one to chase after them, rather than the other way around.

This mind-set trickled down to even how I presented myself. If I was getting ready for an event, dinner, or social gathering, I made sure I dressed in a way that others would find admissible. I didn't want to wear heels if I knew the other girls would be in flats. I dreaded them thinking I was overdressed. Or I shouldn't bring my designer handbag because then maybe they would think I was a snob or not easily relatable. Moreover, perhaps I really should break out the high-end accessories I did have so that group of women would believe I was "chic enough" to hang. The way I dressed, what I purchased, or how I carried myself entirely was all dependent on what others would think of me. I could put an outfit on and feel that I looked pretty rockin' in it. But if I believed they would maybe think it was a bit extra that I was wearing a dress and they were wearing khakis, I had better just skip it and wear something else. Let's pause for a brief intermission.

My greatest fear within this discussion is that you will misunderstand me and you will accuse me of being inconsiderate of others. This is not a rite of passage to become a savage woman being uncaring or inconsiderate toward the rest of society. I am quite opposite of that in that I love people and I serve a God Who calls me to love others immediately after loving Him. I will never be the girl to throw up two-piece signs and not give a rip about if I've harmed you because in all reality I am ever so tenderly looking for ways to love others to lead them to Christ. The difference in me now is that I like myself enough that I don't have to wait until others do too. Let me explain what I am babbling on about.

There was this one time around Christmas when I was invited to my boyfriend's friend's holiday party. There was a generous mix of both men and women there, and I had met the females of the group prior just one time. In that brief meeting, they had no time to socialize with me, so I deemed this as our first legitimate interaction. I had no idea what to wear being it was a house party, and I stared at my closet trying to figure it out for roughly a half hour.

I reached for my favorite pair of jeans, grabbed a new nine-dollar top I had bought myself that previous week, and put those clothes on my body. I looked into the mirror, and I decided that I needed a belt. As I opened my closet and reached for the box that held all of my belts, I saw my brown, leather, American Eagle belt. Then I saw my Gucci belt, and my hand tossed to and fro. The old thoughts crept through my mind about what the girls might think if I wore Gucci. Snob, gold digger, and stuck-up were just a few of the stigmas I assumed that they'd attach to me. As my hand reached more toward the left, where my comfortable, very worn-in leather belt from AE lay, I cocked my head to the side, crinkled my nose, and puckered my lips. "Nah," I said, "I'm going with Gucci."

Guys, most of my pinnacle realizations are cultivated by such insignificant moments. Deciding that I would wear that belt, that $530 belt, made me want to high-five myself in the mirror. I remember walking into the house that evening and getting the up-down look we ladies are often guilty of giving each other, and I made sure my double "G" belt was highly visible. Heavens forbid if you believe for a second that it was because I wanted to show it off. There are in fact expensive things I've treated myself to because I work hard and have earned them, and then about 40 percent of the rest of my closet comes from Walmart. Can someone say, "Amen"? It wasn't about the belt or the socioeconomic status that did not directly reflect my financial means at all that made me proud. It was for the first time, the very first time in my life, I did not care what those girls thought of it. And it wasn't about them personally, although they served to be the pawns in my game of defying people pleasing for that evening. It was about the girls who whispered when I was the new student in elementary school. It was about the times I wore a one-piece bathing suit because I didn't want to wear the bikini I loved in fear of what they thought. It was for the girl who constantly tamed her sparkle just to not dull another's. It was for once about me and not about them.

For years and years I let friends and different guys completely take advantage of this submissive nature which lowered my standards. They knew who I was. They knew I valued peace and acceptance over everything else that they used it to their advantage. Mind you, I never succumbed to peer pressure when it regarded something that went against the law or my faith. If people around me were getting into trouble, I was off the scene quicker than you could say "goodie-two-shoes." I'm proud I had those limits. But as for the other factors in the equation, when it came to not celebrating that I made cheerleading captain because I didn't want the other girls to be angry with me, that was just weak. But then, life happened. I got a bit of mud slung at me, and some people really stinking hurt me. Everyone has a breaking point. We see that with water when it finally reaches the point of boiling. It cannot help but begin to erupt. So rather than completely erupting, I began to simmer. After looking at my reflection and seeing all the dirt others had left, I got tired of it. I got tired of others' dust clouding my own judgement of myself. I mean more. You mean more. I was very good at saying, "I'm sorry," but now I'm even better at saying, "Accept me."

Let me remind you again because it's *that* important. I'm not sharing these ideas with you to turn you into some rebel rouser who defies the rest of mankind. I'm not looking to be your coach leaning over you rubbing your shoulders egging you on to take your opponent out of the ring. Nor am I trying to turn you into some bad-butt tough gal who doesn't care about what anyone thinks of them. News flash: You'd have no friends if that were the case. What I want is to scoot you from that one extreme of making yourself miserable at the expense of others and find that nice, little sweet spot of balance. So here is how we are going to do that.

I want to take you on a walk through a quick recovery plan that has helped me. Consider it a race track, being that you will circle it again and again, because this isn't going to be a one-time learned lesson kind of deal. Nonetheless, on your mark, get set, let's go!

You can say no. Go ahead. You are allowed to. So many of us are afraid of telling others, mainly the people we love, that short yet bold, two-letter word. Come on and practice it with me right now. One, two, three…no. Feel good? "No" is not some evil word that you feel you should choke on when admitting it. Behind that word sometimes lies self-care and a whole lot of self-respect. The issue is that fear if we tell someone no they are going to be displeased with us, or perhaps if we decline, they will find another person to fulfill our place. Even worse, if we forgo, we've let that person down which in turn makes us feel like garbage about ourselves. Here's the deal, girl. Sometimes saying no to them is saying yes to you. I don't care if it's a matter of staying home in your mismatched pajamas eating cookie dough rather than attending their plans or declining volunteering at one more stinking event because you are just too tired. Maybe no for you means finally saying, "No, I mean more than what you've been offering." Regardless of the situation, I encourage you to respect yourself enough to say *yes* to saying no.

Moving ahead, as no is something you should practice saying more, "I'm sorry" is something you may need to start saying less. I used to love apologizing when I had nothing to be sorry for. Someone could be blatantly rude or spiteful or do something that totally hurt me, but I was the one to offer remorse just in hopes that we'd be in good standing again. I mean, how bizarre is that? Let me put it this way. If you have someone over for dinner and they drop one of your favorite dishes and it breaks, are you going to apologize for having a dish out to begin with? No! In the normal, expected etiquette of what makes the world go around, the person who dropped the plate, the faulted, would apologize for having broken your dish. It makes sense. So if someone decides to ignore you, to gossip about you, to slander you, or to cheat on you, girl, why are you the one apologizing? I have always taken pride in my character that I am very easy to say sorry. If I know my temperament has been off or I did something that was hurtful, I lower my pride all the way to my toes and extend my heartfelt, sincere apologies to whomever I harmed. I take joy in doing so because I know that I am a human and I am in dire need of grace. But if I'm willing to belittle myself in efforts just to salvage a relationship, I'd rather say, "Sorry I'm not sorry."

Next, and this one may be difficult to digest, but you are not ice cream, puppies, or coffee. Not everyone is going to like you. Oh, this tidbit is my favorite. I want you to immediately shift your attention to Jesus Christ for a moment. Think about Who He is and what He has to offer. This perfect, holy Savior came to this earth, lived a sinless life, yet died a sinful death, conquered hell, and was raised from the grave for you and me. His sacrifice offers eternal life for us, the ones who do not deserve to even stand in His presence. Yet there are people in this world today who absolutely despise the mention of His name. They detest Him. Think about that for a moment. You are flawed, you've messed up a bajillion times, and you've hurt others. I have done so more times than I can recollect. So if people can refute the Savior of their souls, Who loves them with an incomprehensible love, what makes you think that the whole world is going to like you too? Now please, I pray you've not been harmed by my words, but it's the truth. Remember I said before how I would obsess over one single person not liking me? There was a girl I went to high school with who worked at McDonald's, and I'd always interact with her when I went through the drive-through. We grew up together and saw each other daily, but now she acted like she never knew me. It irked me beyond what you could imagine. I would pull away, and before my window was completely closed, I would frustratingly exclaim, "What did I ever do to you?!" I truly had no idea why she continued to pretend we never knew each other, but I had to accept that. If I knew there was something I should have apologized for, I would. In fact, if you are reading this now whom I am speaking of, I am sorry if I ever offended you. However, I am not going to waste another second before my French fries get cold worrying about approving myself over someone else's feelings concerning me.

Carrying on, you must know that it is more than okay to agree that you disagree with others. I used to never, ever express my opinion concerning anything if it differed from the people around me. Granted, that never pertained to Jesus. He is my one thing I will go kicking and screaming defending with ease. I'm never going to silence Him to blend in. I'm going to radiate Him to bring others *to* Him. I just wanted to remind you of that. However, if I was discussing a recipe, a celebrity, the new gym regulations, or a restaurant, whatever you say, I'd be your doo-wop in the background. I could love a restaurant so much that they would name a dish after me, but if others around me disliked the place, I'd nod my head and admit that it wasn't that great after all. Let me tell you something: Your opinion matters. It may not be liked, it may not be valued, and it may not even be respected, but it matters. You don't have to be a big, bad disagreer or contradict everything anyone says because that's not necessary either. But I need you to grasp that just because the crowd doesn't go along with you doesn't mean you are a loner. You are not playing a game of chicken anymore, and we are no longer in the business of swerving ladies. You plant your feet and stand your ground, because you are important enough to be heard, and it's better to stand out than blend in. We're almost done. Don't bail on me yet.

Lastly, I pray you understand that you can do all of these things and still be a good, Christian girl. I feel as though as you are reading this you may believe I am defying the reputation of Christianity, as though I am encouraging you to be a mean girl. Remember when I started this chapter I admitted this was the one I feared you'd misconstrue me? This is why. You can say no and still be kind. You can not apologize when you've done no wrong and still be genuine. You can voice your opinion about whom you voted for on *American Idol* and still have good judgment. Being a Christian never meant being passive. In fact, if we were to be that way about sharing the gospel, how many people would we reach? Jesus never begged anyone to love Him. He's a gentlemen. He says, "Here I am! I stand at the door and knock. If anyone hears my voice and opens the door, I will come in and eat with that person, and they with me" (Revelation 3:20 NIV). He was boldly Who He was, represented everything He came to be, and didn't apologize to anyone along the way. He didn't fear if the Pharisees would be offended if He healed people on the Sabbath. He wasn't afraid of extending a hand to the adulterer before the stones were to be thrown at her. Jesus is valiant and was unapologetically Who He was, though He acted in love. That's us too, ladies. We can be bold and brassy, and we can have enough self-worth to defend ourselves to others all while operating in love and kindness.

When I began to step outside of my comfort zone and promote things, I was ridiculously concerned about what others were going to think about me. What if they become annoyed with me, what if they disagree with me, or what if they unfollow me or unfriend me on social media? How am I going to feel if they completely turn me down? I was so fixated on this smaller circle of people accepting me that I had no idea of this amazing, supportive, incredible group of women I was about to connect with. When I started influencing for a t-shirt ministry called The Light Blonde, I honestly thought I was in over my head. The opportunity presented itself online, and they were accepting applications for being a brand influencer. I had already had a cubby full of their t-shirts, and I thought, *Sure, why not?* I applied to become an influencer, and within a few short days, I was surprised to be notified that I had been accepted. Immediately I was super pumped that a gal with only 430 Instagram followers was accepted to promote a brand I love and be a part of a ministry with a following of hundreds of thousands. I would be taking something big, something so beyond me and awesome, and promoting it to this little pool of people whom I had already assumed was not going to be as excited as I was; and that kind of freaked me out. But do you know what? I did it anyway. I didn't worry about what they thought or if I'd be chalked up to another sales person on social media. I simply did something that made me happy. My reward you may ask? I took a giant leap proving to myself that I can do something for me and not worry about if it impresses others. I learned that if the crowd I'm in front of isn't a fan, there's always another audience willing to applaud me. I gained an entire network of incredible women who are supportive, kind, and accepting. So if you have been wasting your time trying to please the same people as I did, perhaps it's just time you change your circle.

The last discussion I want to have with you is revisiting the Bible verse I included in the beginning of the chapter. Go ahead and skim a few pages back to refresh it. I'll wait! Notice the last sentence of that verse: "If I were still trying to please people, I would not be a servant of Christ." That's deep, guys. There was no beating around the bush with Brother Paul. He unashamedly stated if you are pleasing people, you're not serving Christ. That's confusing, I'll admit. Do we interpret him to have said, "Hey, you know what, guys, just forget about mankind. They stink anyway, so who cares about them?!" Of course not. You and I both know better. What he is suggesting, though, is God first and others second. The only permissible time I can tell you that is completely acceptable regardless of me knowing the entirety of your situation to put someone else in the second, third, or tenth place position is when it comes to Him. He comes before your spouse, He comes before your kids, He comes before your dog, and in fact He even comes before yourself. You can make your friends happy, but if it doesn't make God pleased, then what have you gained? Would you really consider it "winning" if someone else was happy about what you've done to make them so, but let God down in the process of doing so? I hope not.

So in sum, let's take a giant step back from the habit of going through your mind over and over again about what you said and how you said it or wonder how they interpreted it. Stop over worrying about if they are mad at you, if you disappointed them, or if you hurt the girl's feelings for saying you like her new haircut better than her last. And stop, sis. Please stop worrying about pleasing everyone else in this world more than your God and more than what makes you comfortable. Remember Jesus didn't wait for the approval of others prior to becoming everything God called Him to be. So neither should you.

Things to remember:

- I cannot make everyone happy. Repeat several times.
- Changing who you are in efforts to make others happy will leave you unhappy.
- It's okay to have haters. Jesus has them too. Just don't hate back.
- Do not do or not do something because you are waiting on people to approve of it.
- If Jesus approves, but the rest disproves, you still made the right move.

After reading this chapter:

Something that stuck with me is…

_____

_____

_____

_____

_____

Something I want to challenge myself with…

_____

_____

_____

_____

This is how I am going to do it…

_____

_____

_____

_____

My I Am Her statement is…

_____

_____

_____

_____

Chapter 10
The Obsessive Planner

Many are the plans in a person's heart, but it
is the Lord's purpose that prevails.
—Proverbs 19:21 (NIV)

If you spend too much time planning, you might
not have much time left for starting.
—Andre Dominguez

I sniff books.

I know. Weird, right? Let me tell you something even more peculiar.

Every time I purchase a new book, I have a regimen. Let me preface with the fact that I love physical, tangible copies of books. Don't get me wrong. I dig the Kindles and e-formats (especially if you're reading this via one of those channels now), but I have this thing, this routine when I am holding a new read in my hands. First, I open the book to any old page. I then stick my nose right in the center of the binding and take in a big whiff and then grin as I exhale slowly. If I could bottle up the smell of books, I would. I'm not sure if it's my passion for written words, the nostalgia of the simple yet lost love of reading, or just another thing that makes me Gabrielle; but I absolutely savor the scent of them. Next, I skim to the last chapter of the book and flip and flip. Ah, the last page.

I read it.

Yep, I read the last page of the book, then go to the first one, and begin the novel already knowing how the story ends.

Don't ask me why. Don't try to understand because I myself cannot explain why I hold such an odd tradition. Perhaps it's my anxiety and loathing the unknown that I find contentment in being prepared as to how the story ends. Maybe it's just a surface-level, strange quirk. But I can't help myself. I love to possess the control of knowing and predictability. It's my thing.

I have always been a fervid, obsessive planner. If I summon an idea in my mind about a plan, you can bet your tomorrow that I have assigned a strict, though very detailed itinerary about how it is going to commence. I will compose a time frame, a budget, products, cost, who's driving, what type of snacks will we be indulging, and optimal times for bathrooms breaks before endeavoring any expedition. I know it's a bit extreme. I can be exhausting, you know.

Say, for example, my annual New Year's Day tradition. On the first day of each year, you will find me eating sausage and sauerkraut in front of my MacBook Air anxiously creating a financial spreadsheet. Honestly, I am surprised smoke doesn't lift out from underneath my fingers due to the ferocious typing of my well-thought-out fiscal planning. I list every single paycheck I will receive from January 1st until December 31st of that upcoming year along with every bill and provisional celebration such as weddings, birthdays, and baptisms—you name it. I budget like I am managing the finances for a national banking institution. Of course I slap a giant, bold, all-cap GOD WILLING on the top of my spreadsheet, as I am aware it will change throughout the course of the year; but believe me myself and my bank account are more than prepared. We are ready.

I then tuck that crisply printed, color-coordinated chart into a shiny, smooth protective sheet that nestles into a clean, white binder. In my eyes, I have a financial plan, and I am sticking to it. I am content. I am secure.

But then it changes. My original plan that I spent quite some time so strategically orchestrating alters even in as short as one month. I did not account for suddenly needing new tires on my car or a surplus because of a bonus I received at work. There was no projection that certain instances would befall to disrupt my beautiful, well-thought-out itinerary, but nonetheless, it happened.

And similarly, such is life.

When I was sketching the exterior design for the patio furniture on my back deck, I had no idea that in all actuality, I wouldn't even be living in that home in just a few short weeks. I would stand in front of the sliding glass doors that led to our deck and measure and idealize which piece of furniture would fit where and who had the best deals to bring my designs into fruition. I would put a flower on a tiered plant stand in that corner, opposite of the heat lamp, and I would need approximately fourteen stair lights to illuminate the steps leading from our backyard. Joke was on me, though, because before the snow melted off of the posts of my deck, a For Sale sign was in my front yard. That deck would soon not even belong to me any longer; rather, it would become a stranger's. I planned, I strategized, I made charts, I had lists, I had dreams, I had a vision, I had a filled online shopping cart, and it all came to an abrupt halt because life figured otherwise.

I was dumbed, perhaps even foolish. How arrogant I must have been to plan so far ahead, I thought, when my dreams did not even slightly resemble my updated reality. The budget, the designing, the ideas—they ended up in tiny misshapen pieces of paper at the bottom of a trash can. My plans had different plans after all.

It's incredible how quickly our focus shifts when presented with unexpected instances. The only piece of furniture we had on our deck was this little square table with four blue chairs. It was an adorable, sturdy little table, and it was dear to me because my mother surprised me with it when I couldn't afford to purchase one prior to my wedding. It meant a lot to me. So many times I would stare out the kitchen window at it as snow collected on its surface, and I would think, *I'm going to need to expand that one*. I would envision myself having to accommodate all the guests I planned to welcome into our home. Then there came a day when a stranger knocked on the front door of my almost empty house that I almost did not own anymore, who said, "Hi, my wife sent me to pick up the patio table we purchased." I stared at him numb, like a robot, and said, "Right this way, sir," as I led him through my vacant home. We conversed as I helped him fold those blue chairs and collect them onto his truck, and I trembled as I watched that little table and four chairs drive away. Isn't that how life works, though? We take things for granted, like a little table collecting snow and debris from the winter. Then we lose them and then yearn for their return or the stability of their presence. What was happening? I surely didn't plan on this.

Each mishap I've had in my life, let's say, for example, break-ups or heartbreaks (yes, those are two different sorrows), I've found myself in the same position of questioning God. How many evenings I've spent bartering with God Almighty spewing out that I believed I had followed His presumed plan for my life, but why all the shambles? Why was I facedown in the thick, clumpy mud, nose buried into the dust of where I had fallen? Frustration would flow from my spirit as I would haggle with God that I believed I was planning right, I was following right, and I was believing right, so how did everything turn out so wrong? Why did my course take a detour on some rocky, beaten path that ended in a "No Outlet" destination? Surely speed bumps and roadblocks shouldn't be included on the map of the journey of my life, right? Eh, wrong, sis.

Sometimes the bumps really *are* intentional. And oftentimes, the very bumps that send us off-road are the catalysts that lead us to rerouting.

Can I refresh you with something? God's will includes the unplanned, unexpected, sometimes-not-so-fun occurrences too. You didn't think it was coming, but God *knew* it was.

So very often we believe that the nasty parts of our stories are not God's will because how could a bad situation come from such a good God? Isn't that the epitome of the debate of a fallen world wondering, *How can such a good God allow such bad things to happen?* We've all been there. Whether we'd like to admit it or not, being it may taint our faith meter as a Christian, we've all admittedly asked ourselves, and God at times, "Why?"

When I sit down to happily organize my yearly budget, He knows it's entirely adaptable. I even know that, though I rigorously plan nonetheless. As I scanned the countless online pages of Wayfair.

com to select my new outdoor furniture, He knew that would no longer be my address anymore. When I continued to send my resume to my dream place of employment prior to college graduation, He knew I'd never even cross the threshold of that building. The dream dress I wore down that aisle that I imagined I would God willing pass along to my daughter one day, He knew it would end up in a ball on the dusty floor of a storage unit. You're getting the idea, right? He knew, He knew, He knew it all. I had plans, and I didn't appreciate them being interrupted. That's why I planned them, duh! His plans wrecked mine. But praise be to God, because His redirection was my resurrection.

Go ahead. Read that last line again. I'll wait.

When God so graciously, so gently unraveled the plans I unknowingly tangled myself in, He redesigned the mess I had made into something that looked picturesque again. And He did it with love, humility, and grace. He did not condemn or convict me for my wrongdoing or ill-planning, nor did He do an I-told-you-so dance on the golden streets of heaven. He just picked me back up, brushed off my shoulders, and set me on my feet again. Little by little, I began to see why He lifted me off of one path and led me along another, on the higher grounds. The road that I planned and the one that He planned often ran parallel to one another that as I traveled down His, I could see the destruction and devastation mine was heading toward. And then sometimes, rather oftentimes, it was left as a mystery as to where I would have led myself to. Truly, I did not need to know. I could see how that job wouldn't have been right for me, that man wouldn't have been good to me, or that agency would have misrepresented me.

In our human capacity, we can only see the result of our actions in the present state. We make a decision, and immediate results are what are perceptible to our eyes. Our society is all about instant gratification. Results must be produced at once for them to be worth our while. We've become so obsessed with the "now moment" that we are in and want to construct and plan our now to evolve into our dreamt future. And let's face it. We like to stick to our schedules. Who doesn't? However, what we fail to realize is that God does not only focus on our right now; rather, He is much more concerned with where we are destined. While we focus on the current, He is tending to the details that trickle from the momentary ones we've already established. He is interested in the results long after their immediate attainment. We wish to land a job, but He is concerned about the career. We hope to have a wedding, though He is invested into the marriage. You and I pray to have a house, but He knows where our home resides. He is busy managing the details of our lives that you and I have not even had a fleeting consideration of yet. That's just how strategic, and loving, He really is.

The devastation of my failed plan for a lifelong marriage was a sizable eye-opener for me to come to grips with this concept. You guys should have seen me. I actively utilized roughly three planners at a time and carried one in my purse. I actually planned on sitting down to plan. It was outrageous. The many evenings following my sepa-ration with my ex-husband spent with tears streaking down my face and body jerks of sniffles gave me ample time to do some self-evalu-ating. If you don't use epic circumstances to alter your being for the better, you are allotting that entire experience to be completely taken in vain. I strenuously flipped through many pages of notebooks with well-thought-out plans and scanned through my joint budget binder he and I had together, and it tangibly became evident to me that I had a real issue that needed my attention. In fact, had I not made so many plans, it wouldn't have been so incredibly difficult to give them up. Now I'm not talking about dreams and goals and lifelong aspirations. No, girl, you write those puppies down and stare at them every day. Affirm your dreams to yourself until they've become your reality. I truly encourage you to do so. But writing down a grocery list for an entire month? Can we say #extreme? Nevertheless, I was disgusted with planning altogether now. I needed a clean slate.

The changes I began to make in my life were extremely subtle, perhaps quite invisible at first, but they were monumental to me. I began to exercise the phrase we as Christians often struggle with so much, "Your will be done, Lord."

Maybe you don't have as much trouble with those five words as I do. Perhaps you are a VIP Christian who juggles those words around effortlessly. I applaud you if so. Truly, I do. Quite honestly, I envy you for that, because that was always something difficult for me to proclaim. It wasn't that I didn't trust God or because I believed that He didn't know what was in all actuality the best will for my life, but because I didn't care much for the methods in which He operated. I could perhaps agree with His destinations, but not the journey He mapped out for me to get there. Take for instance again the growth and spiritual maturity I acquired through the season of divorce. That experience composed a substantial part of my character, but I abhorred that journey. It was unboundedly difficult, but painstakingly strategized to work for my greater good.

I began to look at all the plans I had in my life whether it be marriage, finances, career, books, endeavors, brands, marketing, and so on—let your imagination run wild—and I developed somewhat an "I don't care attitude." Now let me briefly vindicate myself. It wasn't an insensitive, realistic I-do-not-care mind-set I instated, but rather a shift of who was doing the caring. My cares became His cares. The more my plans failed, the more I saw His prevail. Even if it took some time for me to discover that truth, His were and still are always better than my own. God's always right, gals. Accept it.

So now, when it comes to, say, money, here is how I roll. I will always, and I do mean always, be an avid steward of money. That's an inept part of my being, and I take great pride in that knowledge and wisdom God has given me. The difference is I do not obsess over planning it any longer. I save money, but tormenting myself over my utilization of it is no longer my god. If I want to buy a new outfit and I didn't budget that in for the month, I allow me to bless myself. I treat myself in a responsible manner (note that I am not encouraging you to go rack up a charge card in the name of this book), and I enjoy the fruits of my labor. And my wallet, well, that's just a small token on the large scale of my life that I do not obsess over any longer. If I don't make it to the gym, I'll get there the next day. If that dream guy becomes a nightmare, I'm sure there will be another. And if I don't adhere to my time constrained scheduled, tomorrow is always another day. Breathe. It will happen, when it happens, if it should happen.

Here's the bottom line. Plans are great. They are beneficial, and we all prosper from organization. When I was in fifth grade, I would stare at this short but powerful quote my teacher had paraded across the front of her classroom. "Organization eliminates confusion." Mhm, preach—it really does. But if we become too obsessed with plans, we actually begin to commit the sin of idolizing knowledge and control. You and I were never meant to be predictors of the future. God gives us the gift of time because He knows our human fragility can only handle so much in a measurable amount of minutes, hours, days, and years. It's like a protective bubble He has placed around us for our own good, but we poke and poke and jab and try to make holes so we can peer into the future.

Stop poking, girl. Put the stick down, drop it, and be still.

You need to know this. Your heavenly Father is entirely aware of your wants, your desires, your dreams, your goals, your needs, and the resources required to obtain them. And sometimes that means loving you way too much to not give you what you want, but instead to give you what you need. Even when that does not look desirable to us, even when it's not the way we wanted our cookie to crumble, the final word is that His better is our best. It's okay to not know what's next. It is all right if you have no idea where you are being led to in the next chapter of your life. Furthermore, it is completely acceptable, rather preferred at this point, that you do not have your own plan.

As the time grew closer to become eligible to sign my divorce papers, I grew more and more anxious because I knew that meant a shift and change of season in my life. While I was still legally married, though having no idea where my husband physically even was, I was on pause. I was safely able to do absolutely nothing but sit, pray, trust, and wait. I knew once I signed on that line, though, that I was getting off the bus of that journey and staring at a map of roads and would have no direction where to go. But I knew that whatever bus I hopped onto next, whatever road I traveled down, whichever endeavor I would embark, I was letting God take the lead this time. The closer we reside in His presence, the deeper we can focus on just the present. And that's more than enough for you and me.

Of course, on the day I finally signed my divorce papers, I had anticipated it would be filled with fear and sorrow. I had myself mentally prepared and even envisioned my hand fidgeting holding the pen while completing the daunting task. As I stood at the counter of the attorney's office, casually signing a document as if it were my receipt from Hobby Lobby, I felt a release when I curved the last letter of my married name, for the last time. It wasn't because of separation or abandonment or relational freedom. But in that moment, I turned down the pen and slid it over to God. After the young woman behind the desk ended our meeting with "Well, that's it," I walked out of that office with my head held high, my maiden name, and no further plans. And for the first time in my life, it felt good to not have the next step planned.

Sis, there's much to be learned in the midst of your deviated detours and alternative routes. I know it's incredibly difficult and frustrating at times to feel as though you've reached a fork in the road with a crooked wooden sign leading you in various different directions. Enjoy the state you are in, though, even if it's not where you want to be. Pause and ask God what it is He desires you to learn in the moment you currently reside in. Waiting seasons are hard, trust me. Oh, how I know they are. But if we are expected to wait, we must be encouraged to make the most of our time rather than waste it. Ask God what it is that He wants to embed within your spirit during this season. Allow for Him to prune you and mold you into a better version of yourself that you would have never discovered had you not arrived to where you are now. If you feel frozen and without direction concerning the next step for you to take, just scoot closer to Him, and He will reveal where you are to go or what you are to do next. He's doing a work within you in the waiting. And sometimes, we need to be prepared for the very things we are preparing for. Let me say that one again.

Oftentimes, you and I need to be prepared for the very moment we have been preparing for all along.

While you're anticipating the fruition of your goals and dreams and busily planning your many fleets, He is reminding you to take one single step at a time. If you desire to be a wife, He may be teaching you how to become a good one before you meet your husband. If you dream of being a boss babe, maybe you have to learn how to manage little before you are given much. Whatever the dream, whatever its size, oftentimes there are parts of ourselves that need some adjustments and some fine-tuning before we arrive. God loves and values you way too much to let you spoil your dreams by being prematurely exposed to them. And it's worth the wait. He yearns to bless you with your desires as much as you wish for Him to give them to you. And He is a specific, detailed God in that He pays ever so close attention to each one of our hearts' deepest hungers. He knows how to get you there, without any of your suggestions.

Whatever plans you may have, whether they are written in your journal or composed on the notepad of your heart, let us together mark them with a giant "X" and instead write, "Your will be done, Lord." That doesn't mean you forget them, nor do you lay your desires aside. I am by no means suggesting you quit your job tomorrow and negate all responsibilities for the sake of being a free bird. It is good to have goals and dreams and ambition. But rather than obsessing over your plans, just sit back, and enjoy the ride He is leading you on. Leave them at His feet where they are safely rested. I guarantee that you will have no single clue as to how you will arrive, but you will indeed reach your destination so long as you remain connected to Him. And do you know how I know that?

It's not because I know you or your plans or the future.

It's because I know Him. And I know that He gives plans to prosper you and not to harm you, plans for a hope and for a future (Jeremiah 29:11 NIV). That's biblical.

And that, my friend, is enough.

More than enough.

Things to remember:

- Plans change, but God never does.
- Just because your plans failed does not mean that God failed you.

- When you seem to have no direction, give God your complete, undivided attention.
- God pays close mind to the details that you have not yet even considered.
- Ditch the planner and the sticky notes, girl. Let your pen, and hair, down a little.

After reading this chapter:

Something that stuck with me is…

_____

_____

_____

_____

_____

Something I want to challenge myself with…

_____

_____

_____

_____

_____

This is how I am going to do it…

_____

_____

_____

_____

_____

My I Am Her statement is…

_____

_____

_____

_____

_____

CHAPTER 11

The Anxious One

So do not fear, for I am with you; do not be dismayed,
for I am your God. I will strengthen you and help you;
I will uphold you with my righteous right hand.
—Isaiah 41:10 (NIV)

Sorrow looks back, worry looks around, faith looks up.
—Ralph Waldo Emerson

You would think the heaviest part of my being would be the easiest to discuss.

I thought so too. But I was wrong.

Of all of the subjects I could write about, anxiety should be a book in itself. I rationalized that it must be hard to write about because it's just so ambivalent for me that I don't know where to begin. In fact, I saved this chapter to be written last because I knew it would be my greatest challenge of this book. So I'm going to cut right to the chase. I am taking you all the way back to my first panic attack. This is how it all began.

I never had a reason to be anxious. Praise God I never had any traumatic experience as a child and I was loved more than any daughter could ask. That's the thing about anxiety. People often believe that you must have experienced something scarring or endured a terrible childhood to suffer from this disease. That's not the case with anxiety, though. It has no partiality. Anxiety affects the rich, the poor, the young, the old, men, women, and children. Even our pets experience anxiety to an extent. And if you ask me, it stems from one of the darkest corners of the deepest pit of hell.

I was fifteen years old, and it was the month before cheerleading tryouts. This was always a stressful time for myself, because for a fifteen-year-old high school girl, cheerleading was one of the biggest concerns in my life. I never tumbled, but I wanted so badly to be able to do a back handspring. I didn't have to become the next Gabby Douglas. I just wanted to be able to perform a simple backflip. I mean we already have the same name, right? My cheerleading game seemed pretty on point, but the other girls who tumbled had an advantage on me. I asked my mother if I could take some gymnastic classes to reach this mini-goal, and of course she agreed. When I think back to that time in my life, I remember the physical exhaustion I had felt due to the lengthy practices after school. After tryout practice, there was more practicing at a friend's house afterward to perfect our jumps with pointed toes and master our dance routines. I then went to the gym once or twice a week, and I eventually came quite close to accomplishing my back handspring. One evening, though, everything seemed off.

When I walked out of the gym on that one, cold, February evening, something felt different within my body. I had this perpetual fearful feeling, the kind of feeling you'd get if someone were chasing you with an axe in a horror film. It felt like electricity was circuiting through my body and I could not sit still. I had to run. I had to escape myself, but how?

I won't dissect every detail of the days to follow, but I can tell you that I missed the next two weeks of school. I can also tell you that I had to write "1 Peter 5:7" on my hand to get me through the school days once I had enough gumption to return. How would I explain to my friends what I was going through when in fact I had no idea what it was myself? I remember one Friday when school had let out early and my friends had called me at home asking how I was feeling. For all they knew, I was suffering from the common cold. "Yeah, guys, I'm good. I just keep breaking out in sweats and feeling like I have to run to the bathroom because I am terrified. I got some antibiotics, though!" That would surely make sense to other teenage girls, right? I muddled through the next few weeks, and we made it through another year of tryouts. I figured that after those were over and I had made the squad, the anxiety would all just fade away, but it didn't. It got worse.

I spent the subsequent months and years to come fighting this wretched battle. How many mornings I woke up with a pounding heartbeat and sweaty palms wondering where I would get the strength to get through my day. How many college classes I sat through hearing my heart beat into my head while my mother sat in a nearby coffee shop in case I needed her to ride out another panic attack with me. What sounds like hell to endure was peanuts compared to my worst stint of anxiety. I remember the day, and I remember the time. It's etched into my brain. On October 28, 2018, I thought this crippling disorder was finally going to get the best of me. Not only was it anxiety this time but also depression decided to join the party as well. My palms are sweating just revisiting that horrifying time.

I was familiar with anxiety, but a stranger to depression. Let me say, for those of you who have endured or are currently fighting as well, stand strong, my sister. We're in this together. Depression is horrible. It's a thief, a terror, and very-bad-word kind of nightmare. My heightened period of stress caused increased anxiety, which led to depression, which refueled my anxiety, which magnified my obsessive-compulsive disorder, which made my anxiety blow up in flames higher than a forest fire. I was in such a horrible state that I didn't know which fear to focus on at any given moment because there were just too many of them. I was anxious from all the stress, but the depression made me more anxious because I did not feel like me anymore. This time I didn't even recognize myself. I was a stranger trapped inside my own body. I had no idea who I was becoming and if I'd ever have Gabby back. I was horrified.

Being a newlywed, you'd think I was at an all-time prime of euphoria. Our first month of marriage was going pretty well, I had a good career, and I had an absolutely beautiful home and the most loving and supportive family you could search the high heavens for. But that one Sunday evening, after having cooked sauce and meatballs for our Italian-American Sunday dinner, I had a panic attack unlike any other that set me through a series of warfare.

Rather than turn this into a depressing documentary book-marking the days of my sorrow, I want to fast-forward to the meat of this chapter, what I want to gift to you having been a sufferer of this disease as well. The efforts I make within this are not going to be like the others where I'd offer you a tutorial on how to navigate through this multidimensional disease. This would instead be the chapter we would sit across from each other over coffee or Coke and pour out our guts on amble amounts of tissues. So I want to empathize with you and offer you advice that has helped me. In doing so, I want to share some of the lies I've always believed about anxiety and the proof of them being just that—lies from the devil.

Now before we go on, I want to stop and take a quick break for some deep breathing. That's not just a phrase we tell each other when freaking out by the way. A therapist once told me if we cannot control anything else, we can control our breathing. And he's right. Deep, controlled breathing legitimately affects your autonomic nervous system which essentially tells your body, "Hey, it's time to chill out, bro." So let's stop and do that for a moment. From the gut, deep breaths now.

Feeling refreshed? Good! I needed that too after revisiting some painful experiences. Now we are going to get down to business.

I want to address both parties here. If you've never suffered from an anxiety disorder, let me express to you from the bottom of my heart how absolutely happy I am for you. I would not wish such misery on anyone, not on a blade of grass. Maybe reading this chapter will enable you to help someone else who is struggling. To those of you whose feet clenched tightly as you read the preface to this portion, I am here for you. I know that sounds phony because you and I may never have a conversation with each other, but I want you to know that I am here for you in the sense of being in this together. You are not alone, and regardless of all the strange thoughts and feelings channeling through your body, you are not the only one experiencing them. I promise you. That's just one of the many lies the enemy will try to convince you. Here are some more.

You don't need anyone's help. For the longest time, I never wanted any help in dealing with my anxiety. Other than the support of my family, who are also sufferers, I sought no professional counseling because I deemed it unnecessary. I had it all figured out in my mind. I would go into a cold room and lie on a couch with a complete stranger and be expected to open up to them about my innermost feelings. I preconceived in my head that this highly educated, older person with a clipboard staring at me with their eyeglasses halfway down their nose and an indifferent look stuck on their face would be judging my insensible thoughts. I wanted nothing to do with that, that is, until I got desperate. As they say, desperate times call for desperate measures. I remember lying in my mother's bed one morning, and my body felt like it would not even allow me to physically sit up. It wasn't just figuratively that I was at the bottom of a pit. I could actually physically feel it too. In that moment, we decided that I needed to take an additional step, regardless of whether I wanted to or not. I did not even refute the idea; I was hopeless. The first day I walked into the therapist's office, I anxiously sat on a comfortable couch filling out what seemed to be an endless questionnaire. She had informed me after reviewing my results that I could be diagnosed with general anxiety disorder, obsessive-compulsive disorder, and depression. Respectfully, I wanted to say, "Uhm, duh. I know that part already, so fix it!" Therapy didn't heal my anxiety, but it helped it. I was able to look at things from a different perspective and realize that a lot of my disorder was physically induced as well. I'm no doctor, so do not credit me for medical explanations, but it turns out we have this little almond-shaped matter in our brain called the amygdala. In layman's terms, it's the little dude managing your emotions, especially fear. The more I learned about that, the less guilty I felt about all the thoughts running wild in my mind. This brings me to the next lie.

Just stop worrying so much. My therapist explained something to me called an amygdala hijack. According to my own interpretation, it is exactly what its name states it is: a hijack. Nothing makes sense at this point, and your emotional response to what may be a menial circumstance can be taken way out of proportion. It's as though you are not controlling your mind anymore, and your emotions are. When this happens, you cannot just turn your worries off, contrary to what others may be telling you. Mental illnesses are unlike physical ailments, not in the sense that they are better or worse, but that they are multifaceted and rather obscure. My anxiety may look completely different from your anxiety. You might have an extreme fear of being in public places, but I only feel safe within a crowd. Whereas something like high blood pressure is generally just that, your blood pressure is high. Not less dangerous, but we all don't have different types of pressures—it's simply high, low, or right where it's supposed to be. Do not believe the lie that this is something you should be in control of. Remember there's a little almond in your brain trying to figure things out too.

You should be over it by now. I remember desperately crying out to my mother assuming she could peek into the future, "Mom, when am I going to feel better?" One of the greatest things she's taught me about this pain in the neck disorder is "It didn't get here overnight, and it might not leave overnight either." That statement offered me both distress and hope. Shocking how those two feelings can coincide, but they did. I feared how long it would take for me to feel myself again, yet I had hope in knowing that it was "okay" that I wasn't there yet; it just took some time. For some it takes days; for others it takes months, perhaps longer. What you mustn't do is try and force yourself to heal sooner than your mind and body are ready. There is a purpose for the season you are in. I cannot tell you what it is or why you're in it, but I know that there's reason for you walking through the valley. What you may not realize, though, is while you are there, your tears are watering the soil for the flowers to grow. A green thumb I have not, but I do know flowers do not grow overnight.

If you trust God, why are you so worried? I just blew some hot air writing that. This lie really irks me. For those Christians who have told anyone suffering with anxiety that it is due to a lack of faith in God, shame on them. Why don't you ask them why Jesus, Son of God, was trembling in fear when He prayed in Gethsemane? To paraphrase, when Jesus was awaiting His arrest, He admitted to

His disciples that He was overwhelmed with sorrow to the point of death (see Matthew 26:38 NIV). Guys, Jesus was terrified. The Son of God, a blameless, holy Man, was filled with fear to the point of death. Jesus had more faith in His Father than we probably ever will, yet He still was afraid. Anxiety is mentioned in the Bible again and again, chapter after chapter, verse upon verse. It's there. God knew you would struggle with it. He watched His son tremble with it. As He knew you would endure it, He also promised to never leave your side during it. Having anxiety does not make you a faithless Christian; it makes you a mortal.

These thoughts are so real, though. Liar! Sorry. I got ahead of myself. Fear is a liar, and so are all of the thoughts it whispers in your ear. I have been told myself, and even told others, "They are just thoughts. They cannot hurt you." Girl, take that one to the bank. Your mind is such a riveting organ. The human brain is so complex and truly fascinating at what it's capable of. But sometimes, it plays tricks on you, and it can make you feel pretty nasty. My brain would come up with the most realistic, horrifying situations, and I would reside in that panicked mind-set until they actually felt like they were becoming reality. A thought would appear on the marquee of my mind, and that would be the starting point. It was as though my head would say, "Oh, that's a good one! We haven't overthought about that one in a long time." It would then create a little snowball containing that thought and set it on a hill top. As I continued to feed into that thought, it accrued some weight and began to topple off down the hill. The more it rolled, the more thoughts it collected; and before I had time to dive out of the way, there was a giant, life-size snowball coming to roll me over flat like a pancake. I had to stop at the source. When you put out a fire, you don't succeed by aiming at the flames. You eliminate the fire by snuffing it at the base. When a thought begins to surface and I feel as though it's about to take me for a ride, I pump the break and exit before we go off-road. Remember thoughts are powerful, but ultimately that's all that they are: thoughts.

You are so weak. I sarcastically fake laughed the night my boyfriend complimented me for being a strong woman. Strong? Not even close, pal. I appreciated the thought; but how could a woman like me, afraid of her own shadow, be *strong*? Let me fill you in on a few things I learned about strength. First, it's a multidimensional definition. Strength for me might be driving in a large city by myself, whereas strength for you is moving across the world. No one has the right to tell you if you are strong or weak based on their own definition. Second, just because you came home from work utterly exhausted from secretly battling anxious, intrusive thoughts all day along with sweaty feet and a nauseous stomach doesn't make you weak. On the contrary, you got through your day without anyone knowing what you were battling, accomplishing all that you needed to while having a boatload of anxiety. You did it. You did it in spite of everything you had going against you. That is strength. Muddling through a conversation with co-workers, completing your final exams, and putting your kids to bed at the end of the day while silently suffering is the epitome of strength. When I went through my divorce and experienced so very many emotions, anxiety being a top contender, some people would comment how strong I was. I thought they were loony. If only they knew what I was feeling on the inside. What they didn't know is I was feeling extremely weak, but I had a strong God working inside of me. His strength emitted from my being. I'm not weak when I have a God as strong as mine. Can someone shout, "Praise the Lord"?

You are too much work. This lie affected my dating relationships the most. I was never concerned about the love of my family being affected by my anxiety. I knew they were there for me regardless of how I was feeling. Truthfully, they were stuck with me. What worried me most was if the men I was with would love me despite my anxiety. I believed for the longest time that my having anxiety was simply too much work, that I wasn't worth all of the drama. Why would any guy want to put up with me crying over the fact that I have to sleep with a television on so I can hear noise in the background? Quite frankly, I do not care about all of the scientific reasons behind how crucial it is for a good night's rest to sleep in silence. I literally cannot deal with it. My mind runs like a chubby little hamster on a wheel spinning tirelessly. And that was just one draw out of the hat of Gabby's anxiety foibles. Now, I won't get on a spree here to go on about how the right man will love you in all the right ways. Girl, that's a whole other book in and of itself. What I do want you to understand in just a paragraph's time, though, is that you are not too much work regardless of your quirks. We all have baggage, every single one of us. But the right people won't just help you carry it; they'll help you unpack, not just because they're super awesome, but because you are worth that.

I wish I could lasso your anxiety and cast it into a fire to be disintegrated into nothing but smoke and dust. There are no magic words that I can arrange to make your fears fall away as much as I would genuinely love to do so. I cannot do those things, but I can promise you that the light truly does shine brightest in the dark places. I know. I never wanted to hear phrases like that either, but there's a reason we say them. It's the truth despite all of the lies.

Sometimes we don't understand why we go through certain things. Actually, I take that back. Almost every time we experience some type of hardship, we wonder, *Why?* Consider it a seed to be sown, though. Imagine yourself kneeling in a garden on an open ground of soil. For the sake of this exercise, I want you to visualize that your anxiety is something tangible. You bury through the dirt and you plant it and then cover it back up so no one knows where you've set it. It becomes rooted and it grows, but once it breaks through the ground, it resembles something beautiful, something useful. That's the thing with trials. Sometimes, we experience them for others and not ourselves. I've already presumed before those words have even reached your heart that you would question my sanity once reading that, but think it through for a moment. Just as going to law school or medical school is learning how to assist your clients or patients, sometimes learning some difficult lessons is about helping others whom you were destined to reach. That doesn't make anything difficult we go through easier. That doesn't mean you will ever have anxiety all figured out. I would be elated if you wrote to me and said God completely healed you of your anxiety. I know He is more than capable of that. Even if He doesn't, that's all right too. I continue to experience fear, I continue to battle anxious thoughts, and that's just simply being transparent with you. In fact, the fear

I faced in the completion of this book was crazy alarming. I didn't know what would become of it, and I was fearful of having closed the final chapter of something that's become a part of me for years. But if there is always something to be afraid of, then there is always something to be hopeful of too. Let that be your little sparkle, your little lightning bug of faith. Where there is fear, there is also hope.

I pray you are not dismayed because I've failed to give you the antidote to anxiety. I surely don't have the answers, but we must have faith in knowing that we have a God Who does. I am praying for you right now, for every woman whom this book will touch, that God will rest His peace upon you like the warmth of the sun. Hang tight, my sister. Everything is going to be just fine. There are no empty, patronizing words when it comes to what God has to tell you. He doesn't say do not be afraid because life isn't scary. He says it because He is present. He has already visited every single one of your tomorrows, and His presence resides in your today.

If anything else, always remember sometimes your deepest struggles become your greatest triumphs.

Things to remember:

- You are one deep breath away from calming down.
- Jesus was afraid too. Cut yourself some slack.
- You do not need a reason or explanation for you anxiety. Sometimes, it just happens.
- Keep reminding yourself, "This too shall pass."
- You are stronger than this.

After reading this chapter:

Something that stuck with me is…

_____

_____

_____

_____

_____

Something I want to challenge myself with…

_____
_____
_____
_____
_____

This is how I am going to do it…

_____
_____
_____
_____
_____

My I Am Her statement is…

_____
_____
_____
_____
_____

CHAPTER 12
The Work in Progress

Brothers and sisters, I do not consider myself yet to have taken hold of it. But one thing I do: Forgetting what is behind and straining toward what is ahead.
—Philippians 3:14 (NIV)

Forget the former things; do not dwell on the past.
See, I am doing a new thing!
Now it springs up; do you not perceive it?
—Isaiah 43:18–19 (NIV)

You are allowed to be both a masterpiece and
a work in progress, simultaneously.
—Sophia Bush

Yesterday I threw away an entire bowl of freshly made pasta.

I'm not talking about just a portion of it in my personal dish. I picked up the entire serving bowl of a pound of spaghetti I had just cooked, and I threw it right down the kitchen sink. The goal was spaghetti aglio e olio, a dish I had made over a dozen times. For those of you unfamiliar with the Italian cuisine, it simply translates to spaghetti with garlic and oil. I knew the tricks to the trade of this dish, I remembered to double the amount of oil regardless of what the recipe suggested, and I even set aside a cup of pasta water to add later so the spaghetti would not clump together. I poured all of the liquid components into a bowl, added the pasta on top, and transferred my now empty pot to the sink; and when I returned, I had a giant ball of stuck-together spaghetti strands intertwined throughout burned garlic. I knew I was having an off day in the kitchen to begin with, but to mess up a dish as easy as this? I knew better than that. I cooked better than that. Admitting what I had done to you makes me feel shameful that I threw away food considering how many people are without it. That was wrong of me to do. I promise you that's not my habitual routine when I am displeased with my cooking. For whatever embarrassing reason that I tossed an entire meal down the garbage disposal that day I am unsure, but I have some sort of inkling that it has to do with my personal struggle admitting that I am still a work in progress. Although I consider myself a good cook, I'm not a perfect one. I still mess up doing even the things I love most, and as much as it pains me to admit, I am not the upcoming Giada De Laurentiis.

One of the most difficult realizations I've had to accept is that I have not yet arrived. I realize that I am not perfect. We've already been through that a thousand times, and I no longer expect perfection from myself. I'm a master of no trades. Gosh, I hate even saying that. There are things I do well with, some things exceptionally well; but I still continue to grow and continue to learn, and I realize that there is a lot of work to be done in me yet.

When I was in therapy, some of the concepts I was struggling with greatly were the major changes I had just experienced in my world and letting go of my old life. I never lived outside of my home; now I owned my own. I also never lived with a significant other before, and now I had a husband sleeping next to me each night. Waking up without being around my mother and sister was entirely strange to me. Heck, I never even went on a lot of sleepovers when I was younger. The change made me feel like I had even changed. I would rub my sweaty hands together tirelessly explaining to the therapist how the adaptations made me feel so unstable. I wanted all of my old lifestyle back. I wanted to press rewind and hit pause for just a little while longer. She then bemused me by saying, "We don't want to stay the same; it's a good thing that we continue to change."

Flip through the archives of your mind for a quick moment to a certain time when you can admit you were a little bit of a hot mess express. We all have that phase we're a bit embarrassed of. I shudder when I think of my own. My sins, my personality, and some of the irrational decisions I've made make me quiver—especially the stage when I thought blue and silver eyeliner was in. Thank God I have no photographic evidence of that time period. I've even sat down and read some of my writings from years ago including some of the drafts of this book, and I actually laugh at myself for how poorly composed it was. I'm sure in a few more years I will do the same about my current work. I've grown. I've matured. I learned lessons that I was unfamiliar with even a year ago. So thank God I have changed. I know that I'm not where I used to be, but I also know that I have a long way to go and a lot of room for improvement. But for the first time in my life, that's okay with me. I'm not afraid of that. Rome wasn't built in a day, girl, and neither were you.

So now would be the proper time when I'd encourage you with some stories about myself striving for success and finally achieving my goals—how being a work in progress eventually pays off and that there is a plateau you will soon reach where you got a pretty well-rounded idea of how this thing we call life works. You know, really boost your confidence that you are going to gain success in whatever it is that you are working toward. Be your example of how progress turns perfection. I would if I could, but I can't. Actually, I'd rather tell you about my failures instead. I've repeated disgusting transgressions more times than I should be due forgiveness. I've received more book proposal rejections than I could keep count. I've applied for positions I was overqualified for and was even interviewed for such, yet still didn't get selected for the job. I was in a scholarship competition that I didn't even place as a runner-up in. I was not the homecoming queen, and I came in last place many times. I've never successfully stuck to any diet to this date, and I've destroyed many things in the oven even while being an experienced cook. I do not read my Bible every day, I forget to pray before I eat sometimes, and I've been divorced before age thirty. Oh, and I once locked a foster child in a car in the middle of August. Then I hysterically approached a police vehicle screaming for them to bust my windshield and get him out. That is one thing I can genuinely advise you without hesitation. Try not to run toward a police car frantically. They frown upon that. I told you, guys. I'm working on me.

A year ago I would have never disclosed those things to you that I am not proud of, and that's just a skim off the surface of messy Gabby. I didn't want to admit that I wasn't comfortably sitting at my big girl desk in a sharp pantsuit combo just advising others the necessary steps toward having figured it all out. Who wants to share those parts of themselves with the rest of the world anyway? You'd surely never envy those experiences. I bet not one of those instances previously mentioned made you think, *Gosh, I want to be her when I grow up*. But my heart's desire from the first chapter of this book until the last has been to encourage you that despite what we believe the world is screaming at us, we don't have to have it all together. I pray you've got that by now. I want you to feel comfortable enough about every part of you, even the messy parts, that you still walk boldly with your head held high because you have every reason to. And even when you feel like you've learned a whole heap of lessons and made so much progress, there's always room for more. You just have to keep moving forward.

So I want the remaining pages of this book to serve as your personal pep rally. This is from my heart to yours. If I still had any idea where my cheerleading pom-poms were, I would whip those babies out right now and bust a move. Unfortunately, they have been lost to only God knows where, and no one wants to see my poor dance skills. If I even tried to stretch and touch my toes right now, I'd gripe with pain. Also, I only pretend to know what I am doing on the dance floor. I could use some more groove. Regardless, it's about to get rowdy up in here.

Five, six, seven, eight…

I want you to get extremely uncomfortable—heart beating out of your chest, mouth-watering, nerve-wracking uncomfortable. In fact I am going to theoretically push you right out of your seat right now and onto your feet because being comfortable is being complacent. I don't want you sitting on the sidelines any longer. I don't want you lying on the ground tired from being in the game anymore. Now is not the time to become satisfied with where you are. And you did not wake up today to just exist.

Right now you are moving. You may not sense it quite yet, but you are moving forward. I want you to place your hand over your chest and feel your heart beating. You feel those thuds under your palm? That's called purpose. And as long as you have that, you have everything you need to keep carrying forward. "But you don't know what I've been through, Gabby. You don't know how hard it's been." I know life may have been really stinking unfair to you. You might have lost your parents at a young age or been bounced around foster care without any place to call home. You may have been abused or tormented. Maybe you grew up in a toxic environment and endured things you've never spoken of. You were always a day late and a dollar short. Life handed you a deck of cards, and the ones you were given were anything but the winning hand. In fact, you almost folded. But you didn't. There is a time to mourn over what was lost. You are allotted a time frame to grumble and scream and throw your hands up in the air asking why, but you can't stay there. It's time to start moving forward. Take what they did to you, what they said about you, how they hurt you, and that terrible thing that you dealt with and place it in the past now, because it's time to prepare for the new. And it's time to forgive yourself too, or you will remain stuck. Now is the time to embrace what's waiting for you, because what happened to you didn't finish you.

God is continually weaving newness in our lives, just as the flowers push through the dirt and flourish when it's their time to blossom. Just think if the flower refused to bloom because it didn't want to make its way through the dirt. It would never see the sunlight. It has to push itself through the darkness to see the light of day. And no one, sis, no single person on this earth, can make that decision but you. I can give you all the self-help tools and burn your ears with all the pep talks. I can even hold your hand and pat your back along the way, but I cannot be the one to make you press on toward your freedom. Only you can do that. You are not what you've been through. Sure, it's helped make you into the person you are now, but it does not determine how far you can go. Trials are merely stepping stones, not final destinations.

I had a conversation with a foster child recently, and she attributed how well she would succeed in life to her unfortunate upbringing. I asked her to visualize something with me. I told her, "Suppose you are at a table, and someone is handing you two different lives to choose from. One is everything your dreams may be made of. Maybe you go to college and have a successful career and raise a beautiful family. Maybe for you that even means just becoming everything your past told you wouldn't become. Then the other offers you being a single mom left to raise babies on your own cause your baby daddy just got up and left you. You might become addicted to drugs, end up incarcerated because you can't control your temper, or, even worse, be dead long before your time. Which life would you chose for yourself?" She answered me, "Obviously the better one." I nodded my head and replied, "No one is going to give it to you; it's up to you."

And I tell you today, sweet sister of mine, with all of the love in my heart, that it is up to you too. Stop living in the past. Stop replaying the regrets and all that wrong that has been done to you. Stop worrying about what she is doing better than you on your following list. Quit mourning over what you've lost and look forward to what you have to hope for. Stop expecting yourself to be anything more than who you currently are working on. It's okay to be unprepared. God already knows that you are absolutely clueless. He likes you that way, because He loves when you need to rely on Him. But you have to let it go, sis. Let go of what went wrong, let go of the demands, drop the expectations you try to fulfill, and accept that you are still a work in progress. If your hands are filled with old things and prior expectations, there is no room for God to place new ones in your grasp. Remember we're moving now. We are moving from death to live, from fear to joy, from weeping to laughter, from dread to determination, from demands to acceptance; and we're moving from just getting by to abundance. And we are doing that one single step at a time. And that's the joy of not rushing the process or having a deadline to meet. I find relief in knowing that it's still okay that some days I have a hard time feeling good about myself. There are days I still struggle with rejection and make every bit of effort to steer away from anxiously planning my future. I still worry at times about what others are thinking of me or what will happen if I fall short of the expectations on Facebook. I miserably fail to represent Christ, and more than often I find myself growing angry or anxious. I regret that my children will one day know that Mommy was married before, and I struggle with that. I remind myself to this day, still, that I am not perfect and I do not have to be. I am a work in progress, and I accept that. For each of those parts of my story that I've so long despised and hated with my whole being, I'm thankful for them. Those scars are just part of my complexion, and I wear them proudly. That's what made me who I am today. And Jesus loves every single ounce of who I already am. All of those nasty parts of me that I feel are faults, Jesus just sees as windows of opportunity for His strength to compensate my weakness.

You see, my friend, the enemy may play games, but Jesus wins them every single time. He has the final say in the matter; not even you do. So if He deems you worthy of a heavenly crown and a robe of righteousness, if He calls you daughter, you better walk like you're one. If he accepts you as you are and doesn't expect you to have it all in proper order, then neither should you.

Consider this. What would you do for the rest of your life if you knew today everything that needed to be known? If you had a little keepsake box with all the answers written on index cards, there would be no point in experiencing life. You live, and you learn. And then you keep learning. And you keep molding, and you keep shaping, and you keep refining. You make mistakes, you learn from them, and you hopefully don't repeat them. Then again, sometimes you do. We keep working toward this better version of ourselves while knowing there's always room for improvement. That is my passion in writing this book—to be able to speak from an angle of having nothing figured out. It's not that you should distrust me or think I'm a bit goofy, but so that you can relate to me. And here is what I can promise you.

I am not the girl on the mountaintop. I'm not the one that you look up to and view only a sunny sky behind my face as I look down toward you. I won't be extending my hand to you reaching down to pull you up with me. I didn't successfully trek the mountain to reach its peak. When you look upward to see if I've made it, you're instead going to hear someone groaning next to you as I strike the boulder with my own fist trying to make it up too. I'm huffing and puffing beside you, grinning amid our struggles. I'm wiping the sweat beading off of my own forehead as I lend you a towel to wipe your own. I'm tirelessly hanging on by only a thread sometimes. I'm fastening your helmet, rather than pointing out to you that you put it on wrong.

I'm right there with you, with my hand on your shoulder saying, "We got this, sis. We're in this together."

So lift your head, flip your hair behind your shoulder, and admit for maybe the first time ever that you have no idea what you are doing or where you are going. Claim it from the depths of your belly. It will feel good. It's the very beginning of a wonderful adventure for loving and accepting yourself.

Let's say this one together:

This is me. I am her.

Things to remember:

- Your story begins right now. This is your chapter 1.
- You were never meant to reach a point of completion; so keep on practicing.
- You are allowed to not know the next step. Sometimes the greatest adventures were unprepared plans.
- Often the beginning lies long after the journey has already started.
- Never, ever forget He makes all things new—yes, even *those* things too.

After reading this chapter:

Something that stuck with me is...

_____

_____

_____

_____

_____

Something I want to challenge myself with...

_____

_____

_____

_____

_____

This is how I am going to do it...

_____

_____

_____

_____

_____

My I Am Her statement is...

_____

_____

_____

_____

_____

GABRIELLEELISCO

A GIFT

just for you!

Follow these easy steps and
Gabby will send you a <u>FREE</u> gift

1. Open the Instagram app and tap on the camera icon in the top left corner.
2. Make sure the nametag is visible in front of you.
3. Hover the camera over the nametag, then **hold** and **press** on the camera screen until the tag is captured!
4. Click follow, then post in your story one of your favorite quotes from the book!

(Be sure to tag or @mention Gabby in your story)

Gabby will personally contact you for your FREE gift!

***First 100 participants only

ABOUT THE AUTHOR

Gabrielle Elisco has proudly mastered the art of germaphobia, binge-eating pizza, and imperfectionism. She is also a contributing writer for various different Christian ministries promoting the love of Christ. Some of the ministries she has regularly contributed to include Daughters of the King Daily Devotionals, Between the Gardens Daily Devotionals, and *Faith Filled Family Magazine*. Gabrielle also enjoys spending her time being a brand influencer for a vastly growing Christian apparel ministry, The Light Blonde. While not busily writing or promoting the love of Jesus on clothing, Gabrielle performs her daily job as a foster care social worker, where she has served the lives of hundreds of at-risk youth. Gabrielle obtained her Bachelor of Arts in Sociology from Westminster College in New Wilmington, Pennsylvania, in 2014. Some of her published works can be found in *Daughters of the King Daily Devotionals: Volume 1*, *Beseeching Grace: An International Prayer Collection*, and *Faith Filled Family Magazine*. She currently resides in New Castle, Pennsylvania, along with her family. If you are in the area and want to chat about Jesus or puppies or if Ross and Rachel were really on a break over a diet Coke with extra ice, she's your girl.